Give Yourself Permission to Fly

Kick-start your life and fulfil your dreams

Brett Murray

FINCH PUBLISHING
SYDNEY

Give Yourself Permission to Fly: Kick-start your life and fulfil your dreams

First published in 2008 in Australia and New Zealand by Finch Publishing Pty Limited, ABN 49 057 285 248, P O Box 120, Lane Cove, NSW 1595, Australia.

11 10 09 08   8 7 6 5 4 3 2 1

The National Library of Australia Cataloguing-in-Publication entry:

Murray, Brett Alan, 1973-
Kick-start your life and fulfil your dreams.

Includes index.
ISBN 9781876451851 (pbk.).

1. Motivation (Psychology). 2. Self-actualization (Psychology). 3. Achievement motivation in youth. 4. Young adults. I. Title.

158.1

Edited by Jane Bowring
Editorial assistance by Ron Buck
Typeset in ITC Slimbach by J&M Typesetting
Cover and internal illustrations by Chris Morgan
Cover design by Natalie Bowra
Printed by Ligare Pty Ltd

Disclaimer

While every care has been taken in researching and compiling the information in this book, it is in no way intended to replace professional legal advice and counselling. Readers are encouraged to seek such help as they deem necessary. The authors and publisher specifically disclaim any liability arising from the application of information in this book.

Reproduction and Communication for educational purposes

Every effort has been made by the author and publisher to acknowledge copyright material accurately. However, if any acknowledgement has been inadvertently overlooked, due credit will be made at the first opportunity.

Finch titles can be viewed and purchased at www.finch.com.au

Advance praise

'As a professional rugby league player my mental preparation … is just as important as my physical preparation, particularly when some club's football management may perceive me as offering less value to a team than a more higher profile personality.

Brett and I met some seven years ago through my friendship with his older brother Craig, at a time when I was in the middle of my career, clearly at the cross roads. Brett was introduced to me a person who could help me go to the next level in my chosen career.

Brett's enthusiasm and ongoing mentoring has prepared me to deal with life's disappointments and has been a positive influence in my life. Brett's ongoing interaction with me has made a difference to me as a professional rugby league player and a person.'

Craig Stapleton – *professional rugby league player*

'Truly inspiring.'

Peter FitzSimons – *author and sports journalist*

'… The book you are holding in your hands, needs to be in the hands of a young person you know ASAP. Brett Murray is like the cool older brother that captivates his audience with awe-inspiring "Aha!" moments. *Give Yourself Permission to Fly* entertains, inspires and empowers young people to be their best.'

Josh Shipp – *America's teen motivator, TV host and author*

Contents

Introduction

When I was a sixteen-year-old grommet fresh out of school I landed a job as a sheet metal fabricator. I was travelling around with another workmate and our boss building hangers, extremely large sheds, small factories and the like, all across the state. It was pretty cool, at least until the boss decided to stop paying me. But it did take me to some pretty interesting places, one of which was Kangaroo Valley, just west of Nowra on the New South Wales south coast.

One of our jobs was to build a large tractor shed on a farm on the eastern side of the mountain range, just below the peak. The property was beautiful. The farmer and his family lived in an old farmhouse, a little timber structure with vines growing over the small front veranda. We drove past it every morning before sunrise and every evening just on dusk. It was approaching winter so the temperature dropped rapidly when the sun disappeared behind the mountain peak. I can distinctly remember the cosy feeling of that little house as we slowly bumped our way past at about 5.30 every evening looking at the soft warm glow emanating from the curtain-covered kitchen windows. The smoke from the fireplace rose gently into the cool, clear, greying night sky and slowly dissipated into the heavens.

We were working so high up on this property that I felt that I could touch the stars as they came out, one by one, almost like actors in a stage production. This place captured my imagination. Somehow being on this farm on the mountain at this time had an effect that remains with me to this day. I felt energised. I was soaking in the experience and, although I was still only sixteen years old, I was asking questions like 'Why am I here?' and 'Who am I?' and 'What am I to become?'

I was really searching for something in my life. It seems strange, but I can always remember having a feeling, even before I was sixteen, that I was meant for something great, some grand purpose. Having this feeling at such a young age made me feel weird, but as I have grown I have realised that I am here for a purpose, that I have a destiny, a calling if you will, and it's much bigger than me. I am called to fly.

As I have looked back on my albeit short life, I have begun to realise that it is our own choices that determine how high we fly in this world. We can live our lives as one of the crowd or we can go that step further and achieve greatness. If we do, not only will we be a blessing to ourselves, but to countless thousands, if not millions, of others for generations to come. We can become someone whose life becomes the inspiration for others to fulfil their dreams and achieve greatness also.

I run a youth organisation called DARE:Ops. DARE:Ops is totally dedicated to inspiring young people to fulfil their potential and DARE to live their dreams. We do this by running motivational sessions in high schools dealing with self-esteem issues and preparing for the workforce, facilitating week-long 'Bootcamps' and organising and running extreme adventure trips, as well as providing motivational workshops to corporate organisations on subjects like managing teams under stress.

In the past four years we have received some amazingly positive press from television and radio and in newspapers and magazines. An example of this was the publicity we received when we took ten troubled young men on a trip along the legendary Kokoda Track in Papua New Guinea. A major television network did a story on us and broadcast it nationally on their news and current affairs program.

After this unfolded, a second major network offered me my own television series following me and DARE:Ops on another of our extreme adventures through the rugged Kimberley region in north-east Western Australia. The TV series called 'campDARE' was born. This has now been shot, produced and aired. We actually won the ratings nationally on only our second episode!

Who would have thought that I would end up with two of the nation's largest television networks broadcasting my own TV shows – no way! But it happened. My dreams have taken off, and through the journey I've realised one incredible thing: I NEVER HAD TO ASK FOR PERMISSION!

That's the amazing thing!

Most people think that, because of the way society operates, to see your dream become a reality you need permission from society itself to even start to fulfil your dream or achieve your goals. But that is the whole point of this book – you don't have to ask for permission from anyone. If you GIVE YOURSELF permission, you will take off into your dream.

The dreams I have always had in my heart since I was young were to help young people become all they were meant to be and to realise that they are an asset to society, not a liability. The desire to be a phenomenal youth communicator has always been there. My dreams also included one day becoming a champion boxer, having a family and seeing them never wanting for anything.

These are my dreams.

What's your dream? What is it that you want out of life? It really doesn't matter what it is you wish to accomplish, what it is that you desire. You don't have to ask for permission! If you did, the world, those around you, would probably deny the request anyway. There is something that I want to share with you: we've had permission to fly, to see our dreams reach the highest of heights, ever since we were born!

We have permission to fly!

1
Who do you think you are?

Whatever the mind of man
can conceive, it can achieve.
W Clement Stone

What do you think of yourself?

Think of a confronting situation, someone totally in your face, screaming at the top of their lungs, 'Who do you think you are?!!'

This used to happen to me as an apprentice vehicle spray-painter and as a tradesman. It happened to me as a young child in a troubled home. It happened to me at school where I was bullied. It happened to me as a manager of an automotive training organisation, it happened to me as a young candidate in the NSW State election in 2003, it happened in all of the sports I have competed in from surfing and surf-life saving, swimming, boxing, rugby league and rugby union. It has happened to me all my life, and will continue to happen for the rest of it. It happens to all of us in some form or another. The world we live in is always asking the question, 'Who do you think you are?' It is almost as if we have to prove ourselves to the world.

When I speak to tens of thousands of young people each year, I ask this question: 'Who do you think you are?' Some immediately yell out their name, some giggle and squirm, and that's just the guys! Others sit there blankly, kind of waiting for an answer to be given to them.

This is a question that we need to answer for ourselves, though, if we are to see our dreams and goals become reality. We all have an answer, an answer that was developed during the first eight years of our lives, our formative years. Our experiences during these years have a major impact on the way we answer this question.

> As a man thinks in his
> heart, so he is.
> *Ancient Hebrew proverb*

So what do you think of yourself? How do you see yourself? Do you like what you see when you look in the mirror? Most of us see a distorted reflection, a vision of ourselves that has been produced by the upbringing we have had. We often see ourselves through the words or actions of others. Our past can have a dramatic effect on the way we think about ourselves. My past certainly did. Allow me to share with you just some of the events in my life that affected my image of myself.

My past and me

Growing up was pretty hard for me. All my childhood memories of my mum and dad are intense to say the least. My parents separated when I was just nine, and were divorced by the time I was ten. Divorce wasn't very common when I was young, so you were immediately labelled by kids at school as weird. That had an impact straightaway. You came from a family that couldn't keep it together! Unfortunately, in my work today, I can relate to far too many kids that come from broken homes.

During those years of turmoil I was diagnosed with ADD (attention deficit disorder), a kind little label doctors like to give kids who are going through tough times emotionally and who have heaps of energy, like I did. Thank God my mum refused to put me on any drugs. Don't get me wrong – I know there are real cases of ADD. I just think that it is way over-diagnosed, and kids are unnecessarily thrown onto drugs that have clearly labelled side effects like suicidal tendencies. My mother's solution was to simply get me involved in more sport, to keep burning the energy.

Apart from the ADD and being from a divorced family, there were three other factors that had a dramatic effect on my self-image.

I thought I was ugly!

I was on my fortnightly weekend visit to my dad. Dad doesn't remember this incident, as I don't expect him to. The incident to an outsider was negligible. To me, however, it had lasting implications. As children, we remember very clearly the things that our fathers say and do to us.

> Think about this connection with your father for a moment. Your masculinity – unconsciously and whether you like it or not – is based on his. Most men realise (with alarm) that their father's mannerisms, stances and even words are deeply a part of them and likely to emerge at any time.
> *Steve Biddulph,* Manhood

It was on a Friday afternoon and Dad had picked up my older brother Craig and me from school. Dad had a bunch of his mates and their partners from his work over for a barbecue. While they were there, I received a phone call from my first ever girlfriend, Stacey Connors, the love of my eleven-year-old life.

As I hung up the phone and prepared to enter the 'man's realm', the barbecue area, I thought to myself that I had finally done something that would win my dad's approval. I can't remember ever hearing words of affirmation from Dad when I was a young bloke. He didn't seem to have the ability to communicate approval, to say simple things like, 'I'm proud of you son' or 'I'm proud to be your dad' or even 'That's my boy'. Nothing like that was said to me until I was almost twenty. So as I stepped over the threshold to the outdoor patio, I was still seeking evidence that my father was proud of me, that he loved me.

Dad stood with barbecue tongs in one hand and a twist-top beer in the other and said, 'Who was on the phone son?'

This was my chance to announce to the world that I had achieved something manly, something my dad could be proud of me for. You have to remember, I was only eleven! So my proud reply was 'That was my girlfriend, Stacey.'

Dad shot straight back with 'What does she see in you? Can't be your looks!'

I was gutted. Dad was only joking, and I'm positive he didn't mean to hurt me, like many fathers don't mean to hurt their kids. Most just replicate what their fathers did to them. But it does hurt. Words from our fathers can make us feel ten foot tall and bullet proof, or they can make us feel as worthless as yesterday's garbage. As the ancient Hebrew proverb says, 'Life and death are in the power of the tongue.'

Words from our fathers can make us feel ten foot tall

I believe fathers are the most influential person in our lives when we are young. So to any fathers reading this book, please understand the amazingly important role you can play in the lives of your children. It is from you that both boys and girls can get their sense of self-worth and identity. It is from you that children learn how valuable they are. Fathers can show their children how precious they are by standing up for them, protecting them, showing them that they are *worth* protecting. For boys, fathers can also set the standard of who and what it is to be a man when they say 'I'm proud of you son, you are mine.' By fathers taking ownership of their children through word and action, children can receive feelings of worth, value and validity. Now this doesn't overrule the roles mothers play by any stretch of the imagination. Both parents are vital to the parenting process. Unfortunately though, a lot of us grow up without one or the other, or sometimes without both, and that hurts. I didn't realise until just a few months ago that

I had a really poor self-image regarding my personal appearance which I can trace right throughout my teenage years. Looking back through old school books and diaries, reading my scribblings, I saw how many times I wrote about being ugly. After all, without actually saying it, that is what Dad called me.

Bed-wetter!

When I was fifteen, my deepest fear was realised: what I believed to be my greatest weakness was exposed. It was February 1988 and I was attending the Year 10 camp organised by my school, an all boys Catholic college. What was this weakness? I had a chronic bed-wetting problem, something that would haunt me until after my twentieth birthday. Yes, that's right folks; I wet the bed until I was twenty years old.

As humans, we attack as a form of protecting ourselves. We will draw attention to someone else's weakness just so ours is not exposed, but this often comes back to bite us, as I experienced. On the first night of the camp, I had one of my 'little accidents'. In an attempt to draw attention away from my wet bed, I immediately sparked a series of raids with a few mates on the beds of other campers, putting shaving cream and toothpaste, sticks and bark in their beds as a joke. But the joke got out of hand. My mates flew into a frenzy and wanted to keep going, bed after bed, until they got to mine. All of a sudden the lake was revealed. One of my 'mates' then got the loudhailer from the sports master's room, ran back to my cabin, and announced to the 150 participants that 'MURRAY PISSED THE BED!!'

So then I had to spend the rest of the school year being teased daily about my lack of bladder control. The amount of times I was offered nappies that year was ridiculous. The four days after it happened were the only four days in my life where I felt truly suicidal. Weird when you think of it, but that was the effect – I wanted to die. If not for a small voice inside my head telling me it was all right and that I was meant for greatness, I may have done something very regrettable.

Late developer

With all the teasing and bullying I suffered, my self-worth was hammered beyond recognition. However, by the end of the year, another, rather embarrassing, problem had emerged. It was apparent that I was becoming very different from the rest of my classmates, or rather that they were becoming very different to me!

When I left school at fifteen, not only did I see myself as an ugly, known bed-wetter, I was the kid whose voice hadn't dropped yet, among other things! 'Hey choir-boy,' they'd shout at me, 'when's your voice going to break?' I didn't hit puberty until after I turned seventeen. My perception of myself at fifteen was as an ugly, pre-pubescent bed-wetter from a broken home living in relative poverty! Hey, build a future on that, why don't you!

> When I was a child I had learning difficulties
> and I was considered learning disabled.
> I was told I would never read,
> write or communicate, and that
> I would never amount to anything
> and never go very far in life.
> *Dr John F DeMartini*

What others think of you

Other people will always have an opinion of you, and more often than not it won't be the same as your opinion of yourself, especially if they don't like you or are in competition with you. It's a fact of life. Face it – you have opinions about the people around you, so chances are they will have opinions about you. Unfortunately, in today's world, everybody is so concerned about what others think of them that they place more importance on the opinion of others than their own opinions. And what's worse, others opinions and views of other people can actually influence our opinion of ourselves, just as I was influenced by the opinions of others at home and at school.

It's true. Many of the girls I talk to at the schools where I speak are so worried about what others think of them, especially the boys, that it affects what clothes they wear, how they do their hair, what perfume they splash on, even which CDs they buy.

Guys are just as bad; they just aren't as willing to admit it. But their need to fit in – we just want to be loved and accepted – is probably more obvious than the girls'. We think we're being an individual but there we all are in those baggy jeans that look like they will fall down at the first sign of a stiff breeze. I can go to any beach town, any upper class inner-city suburb, any major shopping mall and see countless thousands of young guys, and not-so-young guys, all being 'different' in the same way – the only difference is the print on the boxer shorts that hang out over the top of their jeans!

We worry so much about what others think of us yet the funny thing is that, in the long run, what they think often doesn't help us one single bit. Especially the opinions of those we attend school with. Why won't their opinion help us? Statistics tell us that 95 per cent of school students will have no further communication or interaction with their schoolmates after they graduate. Another reason is that what people think of us generally, will actually have no bearing on us when it comes to life issues that really count, like employment. The opinion of another peer won't come into question when you sit for a job interview. It won't matter what others think of you when you are performing your job, or competing in a sport! So don't worry about what others think – it is overrated!

The truth

Well we're into it now. Are you ready to hear the truth? (Every time I hear that phrase I think someone is going to rip shreds off me, but maybe that's just me.) Here it is as plain as I can give it. Remember that little positive whisper I had among the negative shouts in my head, the one that told me I was destined for greatness? Yes, that one. This is your truth too: you were born a winner! Do you realise that you won the very first race you were in? It was a race for life and death, and you were the sole survivor. Do you know what I'm talking about?

It could have happened in the back seat of an old car or on a beach on New Year's Eve. It might have been during a well-planned romantic evening in New York or Paris, or on safari in Africa. Perhaps it occurred in a bedroom in your grandparents' house, or in the house you live in now. The fact is, the TRUTH is, that when your biological parents came together in an intimate embrace, you, along with approximately 30 million single cells (depending on how fit your dad was), were entered into the race of a lifetime. There would only be one winner, two if biological twins resulted. And out of those 30 million cells, it was you. You were the winner!

Get it? You were born a champion. No matter what you have been told since your birth, you are not a 'mistake'. That comment sucks, BIG time! A 'mistake'? That's just a flimsy excuse from someone who should say, 'I wasn't responsible for my own actions.'

No matter what the circumstances surrounding your conception, be it intoxication, inebriation, intimidation, domination, infatuation, you are an incredible creation. Hello, who won the flippin' race? You did. You are a champion, a winner, destined for greatness, number one, numero uno. *That's* the truth.

> And ye shall know the truth,
> and the truth shall make you free.
> The Bible, *John 8:32*

That encouraging voice you hear from time to time, is your heritage – a heritage of victory, not defeat. *You are not a loser. Losing is learnt.*

Golden Gloves

It's funny. When I run DARE:Ops camps, the most challenging activity for both guys and girls is not the physical exertion we put them through. It's something we call 'Golden Gloves', a great little game I believe every classroom, every corporate business, every sporting team and every family should practise. (That's about the only time you will hear me say with conviction that you 'should' do something.)

Golden Gloves is a game about giving and receiving encouragement. It is about praising someone publicly. Through Golden Gloves I am able to show young people that it's cool to encourage others. I call the game 'Golden Gloves' because in the sport of boxing, in the amateur ranks, the golden gloves champion is the fighter who takes on every person in his weight division and remains undefeated – the best of the best.

The game of Golden Gloves is simple, and I encourage you to implement this anywhere you can in your life. The game is run like this: get a group of people to form a circle. Choose one individual to stand in the middle of the circle. We actually have a set of gold boxing gloves that the person in the middle puts on, but that's not necessary. The only thing that the person standing in the middle of the circle is allowed to say is 'Thank you'.

The funny thing is that most people can quite easily find something they like about another person

Ask each person standing on the circle line to say a sentence, one at a time, about the person in the middle which starts with 'You know what I like about …' (insert the name of the person in the middle of the circle). The key is, each person has to be looking directly into the eyes of the person they are speaking to.

The funny thing is that most people can quite easily find something they like about another person, even if they have only met them a few hours earlier, but the majority of people who slip on the 'Golden Gloves' find it really hard to accept a sincere compliment in front of their peers. Most, out of habit, go straight for the dismissal, or the joke. You know what I mean; we've all done it. The girls are particularly good at it. 'Shaarrtt uuupp' or 'If you say that I'll … I'll … nnoooo doooonnn't please, oh I'll get you for that!'

All that over a compliment! What do they do if you bag them out? But it's true: we have been conditioned to the point where we don't know how to receive a compliment. I was the same until I realised who I was didn't revolve around what others thought of me, it revolved around who I thought I was and what I was made of, and my friend, we are *all* made of good stuff! I began to realise this as I grew older, and I was able to really take stock of my place in the world. When I began to value myself, it became more comfortable to receive a genuine compliment from others. It does take some getting used to, but it's something worth getting used to.

Really, we love to get compliments, and we have to learn how to receive them. I know that I've learnt it from my wife Terrisa. I'm very blessed to be married to a woman who constantly reminds me of how good I look, and how much she loves me. Most people would expect me to say, 'Too bad she's blind!' Well no, she's not blind and I won't say that.

Try it some time – allow people to give you praise. It's a great feeling, and you develop a whole new perspective on the world.

Your choice

You exercise choice all the time. Have you ever stayed up late to watch a TV show or hang out with friends despite

> No-one can make you feel inferior
> without your consent.
> *Eleanor Roosevelt*

the fact that your body is telling you that you are tired and you should really get some rest? Staying up is a choice *you* made. Your body does not control you; you control your body. In the same way, some people choose to smoke, using their addiction to cigarettes as an excuse for not stopping. If you don't want to smoke, then don't. It's a choice you make. I can say this because it is something I have done. I quit smoking through choice, not hypnotism, not patches or gum (although they can help), but I did it through just by deciding to. So did my father and my grandfather. So can you.

I think the most powerful thing we have been given in this universe is the power to choose. We can choose to light up that cigarette, or not to. We can choose to be offended, or choose not to be. So now you have some important choices to make if you haven't already made them. What do you do with the truth? What do you do with the opinions of others? What do you do about your opinion of yourself if it is not the opinion you would like to have?

> All power is from within
> and is therefore under our control.
> *Robert Collins*

What I've learnt

- The truth is that we are all born for greatness.
- Our experiences in our formative years can really have an effect on our self-image.
- What we think of ourselves has a huge impact on what we believe we can achieve.
- We have the ultimate power, the power to choose.

This is who I am: Mohammad

Mohammad was an extremely intelligent young man whom I met in October 2003. He was a proud Lebanese Muslim lad born in Australia who had a quick wit and was never short of a comment or an opinion. All his life he had been called a 'dumb Leb', a 'stupid wog' and, more recently, a 'rapist' and 'terrorist'. Like most of his mates he had a big chip on his shoulder regarding the way they were treated by the general public and the media. He was a straight 'A' Year 11 student at the local high school he attended, even though he had turned up for only 56 days that year. School was just too boring, he said. Mohammad was about to find out there are dramatic ways of dealing with boredom.

You see Mohammad was one of the ten students who came on the Kokoda trek with me in March 2004. Proudly he boasted that he would 'smash' the Kokoda, 'no worries'. But when we set off on the jungle trek that is regarded as the second hardest in the world, Mohammad was faced with obstacles he hadn't counted on. Having to tackle mountains and razorback ridges with 100-metre plus drops either side, dangerous river crossings, heat, humidity, discomfort, and the lack of Mum's cooking and cleaning soon turned this young man from the most confident and boisterous member of our team into the most vocal whinger. He was the first one to say it was too hard, the first one to say he wanted to go home, the first one to get on everyone's nerves – and he was the first to walk into the village of Kokoda!

After he completed the most difficult task he had ever attempted, Mohammad was ready to take on the world in a different, positive, way. His experiences on the track caused him see himself as a custodian of the Digger's fighting spirit, the spirit engraved on the four granite pillars at the site of the battle of Isurava that read: Courage, Mateship, Endurance, Sacrifice. Mohammad began to see himself not solely as a Lebanese Muslim, but as an Aussie with a Lebanese Muslim and a colonial heritage.

Once he began to see who he really was, what others thought about him didn't matter any more. Mohammad went on to top his school in five of his HSC subjects. He then won a scholarship to an elite business college and went on to top his year there. He also became a phenomenal leader in the Lebanese Muslim community where he lived. He became someone who could feel good about himself, and I am very proud of him.

* Terms and Conditions apply: Please see website for more details. Manifestation packages start at $2550.00 (excluding GST and statutory charges). Prices are subject to change without notice, no trade sales. No representations regarding quality, timing or outcome of any manifestation are made or implied. Manifestations are initiated at the sole discretion of the customer, who accepts all liability for damages, actual or imaginary that may result from any manifestation, both now and in perpetuity. Some manifestations rely on seasonal availability of ingredients (and you just can't get good Hamsters in Australia at all) so some features advertised in the brochure may be temporarily unavailable.

2
Go morph yourself!

If I can change, and you can change,
everybody can change!

Rocky Balboa, Rocky IV

Everyone wants to change!

Every person I meet wants to change something about themselves. Whether it's just to become better at something that they are already good at, or to totally change something about themselves that they absolutely despise, everyone wants to change something.

I was one of those kids who used to watch 'The Brady Bunch', totally mesmerised by how positive and understanding Mr Brady was with his kids, never yelling or even raising his voice at them. I would watch Ritchie Cunningham on 'Happy Days' sharing time with his best friend the 'Fonz', who just happened to be the coolest bloke in the world, and think to myself, 'I wish I had someone like that in my life.' I really felt lonely as a kid. So at the age of sixteen, I decided I wanted to be someone who helped people realise their potential and fulfil their dreams; I wanted to be the person I never had when I was growing up. It was during this time when I had the revelation of my self-worth. It was like a light came on in my head – I realised the truth about myself, that I was born a champion. So based on this revelation, I began to change the way I thought about myself, which in turn began to influence the way I acted. I wanted to be positive and begin to believe in myself and my potential; I wanted to achieve my dreams.

Why did I feel so lonely?

When I was young, before my parents divorced, Dad worked a lot, as he always has. I have very few memories of him being at home with us. Mum was always there, but she was busy with housework and working in the aqua fitness industry teaching swimming and trying to fulfil her dreams and goals, along with her own extracurricular activity of netball. My older brother, Craig, was there too, but he was one of those guys who was so naturally talented at everything that you just wanted to slap him! He could dance, run, play footy, soccer, cricket, get chicks – you name it, he could do it. And he did everything better than me, even his grades at school. It was hard being the 'unco' younger brother! We spent very little time with Dad's side of the family – the affection was there, we just never saw them. We had a loving extended family on Mum's side that we spent a lot of time with, Nanna and Pop, and my aunties and uncles, But for some reason, though, I still felt lonely.

I think I felt lonely because I felt different. Looking

back, I realise I thought about things differently to other kids my age. I thought about things that my friends would never have thought about. For example, I would think about how someone who was being made fun of must be feeling. I'd want to say, 'C'mon guys, don't say that. How would you feel if someone said that about you?' But I knew that if I did, I'd get laughed at, I'd become the next joke. And I couldn't risk that; I was petrified that my own weaknesses would be revealed. What if they discovered how insecure I was? What if they discovered that I wet the bed?

And so I became a class clown. I became really good at making jokes about anything, especially other people. It was a case of attack before being attacked, 'do unto others *before* they do unto you'. However masking my fears in this way created a real struggle in me as I knew how it felt to be attacked. I hated myself and I felt even more alone.

Bottom of the food chain

Through my work, I have seen far too many people, young and old but especially young, hating themselves the way I did. They hate the way they look, the way they act, the way they live. They hate who they are, or who they are not! These people see themselves as nothing but a bug – someone at the bottom of the food chain, whose only worth is as a 'snack' for someone else. It hurts me to see people live this way when it is so avoidable.

> The greatest communication skill
> is paying attention to others.
> *Denis Waitley*

I see people from all walks of life not daring to believe they are worth it, not even willing to risk the possibility of failure or the likelihood of success, so they won't even try to attempt their dreams. So many people believe they are 'not' worth it, or they are 'not' worthy. So they live life hiding, hurting, afraid even to dream because if they think of what might be and attempt to achieve it, it would hurt too much to fail, to be brought crashing back down to 'reality'.

Several years ago I was asked to speak at a training day for a certain hamburger restaurant's junior staff and I spoke about self-esteem. I said to the staff: 'No-one wakes up and thinks "I'm a loser!". No-one does that!'

To my absolute dismay, a pretty young girl raised her hand and said, 'Yes they do.'

My stunned reply was 'I've never met anyone who wakes up and thinks that they're a loser, and that everything they do that day will go wrong, that they are simply not worth the effort, that they are not worth caring about. I've never met that person.' I know I had a low self-esteem when I was a young teenager, but I never 'wanted' everything to go wrong!

To this the young girl replied, 'You're looking at her.'

You could have blown me over with a feather! After further discussion, she revealed that she had purposely failed her school certificate and that her opinion of herself was so rock bottom that she believed that she would never be anything or anyone in her life. She was convinced that she was a loser and that was that! She actually hated herself and had tried several times to commit suicide. Inflicting self harm was the only way she knew how to deal with the pain of her thoughts about herself, thoughts that had obviously been fuelled by her experiences and environment growing up, significant adults in her life who must have hurt her physically, verbally, emotionally, or in all of these ways.

Like this young girl, there are many people who don't believe in themselves even enough to allow others the chance to try to help them – they don't believe they are worth helping. I recently met a young Aboriginal man like this when DARE:Ops visited his school in the rural, coastal region where he lives. We put a dare to the students asking who of them wanted to come with us on the trip of a lifetime to the tropical paradise of Western Samoa. All they had to do was fill out some permission forms, do a basic physical with their local GP, get their passports and sit for an interview.

The young man's life had been so torn apart by his negative environment that he simply didn't believe that he was worth helping. We had to work really hard to convince him to sit for the interview. When we asked him why he wanted to come on the trip, he put his head in his hands and mumbled sorrowfully, 'My life is crap! I don't want to steal any more!'

'Why do you steal?' I asked.

He replied, 'So that I can get food for my little brother to eat, because Mum and Dad are always drunk!'

When it came time for the selection announcement, the young man sat in a corner not believing he would be chosen, simply because he didn't think he was worth it, because during his whole life he'd never heard that he was. You should have seen his eyes light up, his chest go out and his shoulders go back when his name was announced. *That* in itself was worth more than anything money can buy. He went to Samoa, surfed some of the best waves in the world, enjoyed Polynesian hospitality, and changed his world view and his opinion of himself! By learning that there were people outside his world who believed in him, he learned to believe in himself.

Change is possible

Like the young bloke on our trip and the girl at McDonald's, there are a lot of people who have a poor view of themselves – who see themselves as nothing but a useless *bug*!

This *doesn't* have to be your lot in life. Do you want to change and grow? Do you know someone who wants to change and grow?

Let's take a look at our friend the bug for a second. While hanging out with my kids, I get to see some really cool DVDs and movies. One of my favourites is *A Bug's Life*, the Pixar classic. One of the characters in this fine animated feature is Heimlich, a heavily overweight Bavarian caterpillar, who some day 'will become a beautiful butterfly'. So you see, even some bugs know that change is possible. They just have to stay focussed. Well, Heimlich was singularly focused. All he did during the entire movie, besides his little cameos in the stage plays with his troupe, was eat! In order for him to become that beautiful butterfly, he needed to eat continuously so he had the energy to go through the metamorphosis. He had to focus.

> ... if you want to become a better you and learn to love yourself, it *will* take single-minded focus.

If you want to change, to morph from being that bug you think you are, if you want to grow, if there are things about yourself you want to change, if you want to become a better you and learn to love yourself, it *will* take single-minded focus. That is how I was able to change myself throughout my life. I have been asked time and time again, 'Why do you do what you do? How was it that you decided to become a youth motivator and a person who lives to encourage others?'

The answer is simple. I decided when I was sixteen years old that I wanted to fulfil my potential. After feeling odd and different during my high school years, I realised I had potential, I had a destiny. I believed I was meant for something better than I had experienced so far, and I wanted to be a positive influence on my world. So that became my focus.

By focusing on being a positive influence, I have been able to establish a fantastic life for myself with a beautiful wife of thirteen years, Terrisa, and three beautiful children, Hannah, Joash and Micah. I own and operate Australia's number one youth motivation organisation. I've been widely recognised through the media and by peers, school counsellors, school principals and politicians as Australia's number one youth motivator. I have produced a documentary for a major television network here in Australia, I have written, directed and produced my own surf movie and, as I shared with you earlier, I have had my own TV series. I have also been nominated for Australian of the Year three years running and I continue to speak to people in the corporate sector inspiring and encouraging them.

This I have been able to achieve by focusing on being the best I can be, but I had to go through different levels of change and growth to get there. Like a caterpillar, I needed to feed myself, and feed myself with the right stuff. If I wanted to be positive, I had to start thinking positive thoughts, read positive material, and spend time with positive people. I had to a make a decision to see the cup as half full, not half empty. But as the saying goes, you are what you eat or, in the case of the attitudes you adopt, garbage in, garbage out. So I maintained the effort and the focus just like our mate Heimlich, and it helped me get to the next level of growth. It is a choice you make!

If you want to change and grow and become a better you, if you want to achieve your potential and see your dreams come true, this is the best advice I can give you: 'Only you can change you!' Other people can give you the tools, but it is you who has the controls, you who makes the decisions. It is not easy, it is not simple, and most of all it is not that quick a process. It really takes a conscious decision to change and constant effort to achieve this in your life.

Thoughts are powerful

It is *your* thoughts, *your* reactions to situations and circumstances that will ultimately dictate where you will head in life. Our thoughts are powerful. What we think affects the atmosphere around us and can affect other people too. I had a friend once who started out as a fantastic bloke, but who somewhere along the way became very negative and bitter. If you hang out with people like this, you end up thinking like them. If I spent a day with this guy, I would come home in a cynical, critical frame of mind that my wife would immediately pick up on and confront me about. She'd say, 'So who has he been complaining about today?' thus reminding me to focus on the positive again.

> Whether you think you can, or you think you can't, either way you are right.
> *Henry Ford*

Vision brings provision

How do we focus on the positive? First we have to set our goals. I hear a lot of speakers and authors talking about setting goals and achieving targets, and I'm all for that. But how do we actually do that? How do we set that first goal? How do we find the motivation to say to ourselves when we're feeling at rock bottom, worthless or unworthy, 'That's it, I'm climbing Mount Everest!'? (Or whatever else your goal might be!)

> But how do we set that first goal? How do we find the motivation to say to ourselves when we're feeling at rock bottom, 'That's it, I'm climbing Mount Everest!'?

The motivation comes from making a decision, from making a choice. Most of the time we are led by our emotions, but we don't realise that our emotions are actually guided by our decisions. For example, if we hear something that could possibly be offensive to us, we have to decide whether we are going to 'take' offence at the comment or not. Notice that 'take' is a verb, a doing word – to take offence you have to actively do something. Imagine that the team you barrack for has just lost to your friend's favourite team. Your friend's side played out of their collective skins, and your friend is going just a little over the top letting everybody know it. You're a bit ticked off as you know that your side played below their best. You have a choice, a decision to make at this point in time. Do you stay quiet and let your friend have his day, gloating over you and your team's loss to his, perhaps even congratulate him? Or do you take offence at your friend's over enthusiastic celebrations? Do you get your back up and make excuses for your team's poor performance? Do you point out your friend's team's poor record and give it back to him?

Could you see yourself in such a situation? Did you feel your emotions starting to get tweaked simply by reading about this scenario? And where do you think this type of discussion would get you? Nowhere, that's where! Wouldn't your friend simply remind you of the cold hard truth: your team lost to his!

After you have made a decision, you start to shift your focus ...

So you see, if you were in a situation like this you would have to make a decision about how you were going to respond and then your emotions would follow suit.

When you move to situations in your life where you have to make bigger, more important decisions, such as setting goals for the type of person you would like to become, you need to make a decision firstly about what you really want, and what you would like to achieve, even if you don't feel you're worthy of it at the time. However, once you make that decision then positive emotions will follow.

This happens because after you have made a decision, you start to shift your focus on making that decision a reality, especially if that decision is about something you have really wanted for a long time. Your thoughts become more focused on your goal and you begin to engage with the processes you need to make that goal happen.

Consequently, as you move towards achieving your goal you begin to feel more positive and begin to believe that you may actually achieve it! These positive thoughts drive you to work harder to achieve your goal and your motivation levels rise, which only increases your positive thoughts even more. That's how you can get your goals happening.

The process of change

This may sound obvious, but it is worth sharing, I think. Positive thoughts produce positive words. Positive words produce positive actions. Positive actions produce positive habits. Positive habits produce a positive lifestyle, and a positive lifestyle, my friend, will produce a positive destiny. The same can be said for the negative. But we don't want to focus on the negative, only the positives.

... once we have made our decision, we then begin to feed ourselves with focus.

Feeding our focus

Transforming ourselves, seeing ourselves change and grow and become a better version of who we are or who we want to be, can only begin to take place once we have made the decision in our mind first. Like the bug, once we have made our decision, we then begin to feed ourselves with focus.

To begin its metamorphosis, the bug has to eat and eat and eat. This begins the process of change. If it doesn't eat the right amount of the correct type of food, it won't have enough energy to go through the metamorphosis.

Now that we have that established, just pause for a second. Are you consuming the right material to help you grow and make it through the change process, or are you filling yourself with junk? The right type of food would be material that encourages you to stay the course of the decision you just made. This might include positive talk, not being involved in negative discussions, and socialising with positive, encouraging people. It may also include watching positive stuff on TV (or not watching at all!), as well as listening to uplifting and motivating music – whatever it is that will help keep you focused. The junk would be the exact opposite, and includes anything in your life that makes you feel negative about your decision or distracts your focus.

Creating a cocoon

The next step in the change process is one that goes hand in hand with feeding yourself the right stuff. Like Heimlich the caterpillar, you need to set up a cocoon, a secure place where you are safe to be yourself, safe to change and grow.

A cocoon can be a place of solitude, but I truly believe for any of us to change, we can't isolate ourselves from others and become loners, because as human beings we need relationships – we are designed to commune with each other. That's why we live in *communities*! To be truly ourselves, we need to express ourselves to others.

Your cocoon doesn't necessarily have to be a place. It can be made up of people too, whether that's one person or a bunch of people. It can be a single friend, a group of friends, your family or your family and your friends. You will know where and who you feel safe with to be yourself. Your cocoon is a place where you are not afraid to say what you think, where you know that what you say will not be turned against you or interpreted in ways you didn't intend. Your cocoon, your safe place is where you will grow. As you are going through the metamorphosis, you, like the bug, are vulnerable to attack, so you need to be surrounded by a protective layer. Now this will take time. Don't think you can just do a backflip and you will have a cocoon, then *voila!* – you've changed! Developing a cocoon takes time. The actual change process is another event altogether.

Some of us develop a false, protective layer, or layers. I know, I used to have them. Remember how I described earlier being the class clown? I would make jokes about the other kids' weaknesses before they discovered mine. I would live by the rule of 'do unto others BEFORE they do unto you!'.

Wisdom involves knowing how to correctly apply the knowledge we have practically to our own life.

Some of our false layers of protection can be made up of intellect or education. We think because we have studied hard we know it all, and we get a sense of pride about ourself because we are smart or educated. We can tend to think that because we know a lot that we don't need to change. Well, there is a big difference between knowledge and wisdom. Wisdom involves knowing how to correctly apply the knowledge we have practically to our own life.

Other false cocoons might be made up of humour. It could be anger, rage, even violence. But these false layers all show cracks eventually and, even if they don't, hiding behind false fronts doesn't help us grow, and it certainly doesn't bring any fulfilment. We spend so much effort maintaining these false walls that we don't have the time or energy to build a real cocoon, a truly safe place where we *can* grow and change to become more beautiful people, without fear of attack.

So I recommend that you get rid of the false layers, the ones that keep people out, and find out who your true friends are. Allow them, through their true love and concern for you, to become your cocoon, and you will find a wonderful new sense of self-worth and self-belief, and the growth process will automatically take off and gain momentum.

> In the middle of difficulty
> lies opportunity.
> *Albert Einstein*

It really is amazing what happens once a feeling of self-belief kicks in. You start to see value in yourself like you never did before. I remember when it all began for me at sixteen. I'd had a pretty hard time in my final year of school, and decided to leave at the end of Year 10. I wanted to be rid of the bullies who had caused me so much grief at school, and I thought I'd rather go out and earn money than go to school. I figured I would earn and learn more in the workforce.

Earn I didn't; learn I certainly did! The school of hard knocks, as they call it, certainly teaches you what they don't in school. In that first year after school I experienced the first of many metamorphic situations that would change my life. I surrounded myself with a bunch of mates, good mates, close mates, along with my older brother Craig, and I began to grow. I began to believe in myself, believe that I had potential, and I *know* that was the beginning of the journey that brought me to where I am today. A paradigm shift had happened; I began to see real worth in me! In the same way, you *can* change your mind about you!

The morph

After the cocoon is set up and the growth has taken place, the next step in the 'bug's life' is the rebirth, the coming of age. This is where the cocoon has done its job, and it is time for a beautiful new creature to see the light of day.

If you have ever seen a butterfly break free from its cocoon, you will have noticed that an incredible struggle takes place. Growth is a struggle! But if you were to help that butterfly in any way through the process of breaking free from its cocoon, you would be doing it more harm than good.

If you were to take a scalpel when the butterfly starts to split the outer layer of the cocoon and slice it open to try to help it out, instead of helping, you would kill the poor thing. Through the process of struggling free, endorphins are released into the butterfly's system that eventually gives it the strength to take flight when its wings are dried. You see, *it's in the struggle for freedom that strength to survive is gained. If there is no struggle, there will be no strength.* It's the same with the birth of a child. With most natural childbirths, the baby has to struggle through the mother's birth canal. This process helps release endorphins and isotonin which help the baby's lungs spring into action once the baby is born. With caesarean babies, the midwife often has to massage the baby vigorously to get the lungs functioning, thus simulating the natural birth process, the struggle.

It's the same when we are released from our cocoon. If someone helps us too much and we don't go through the struggle of growing and learning, we won't truly learn from the experience. Then when we are on our own, and the time of testing comes, we won't be able to realise our full potential. We'll end up relying on the person who 'helped' us 'out' last time. So it will be back to the drawing board, and we will have to learn how to grow all over again – round and round the garden, like a teddy bear! Of course we're not going to die like the butterfly, but we won't get to that new level of growth and change we are after.

On the other hand, once we have gone through that struggle, we sprout wings and fly just like our friend Heimlich. But be careful. It is in this fresh new state of waiting for our wings to dry and become strong enough to take our weight that we are still vulnerable. We have to be careful because we are now in a new realm in our lives, one where we have new possibilities, and new responsibilities. We have to be careful not to go back to our old way of thinking, back to the bottom of the food chain. It is this final struggle, though, that brings about the most strength. When we first step out and experience our new level of self-belief, it *will* be tested. Not so much by others, who often see more potential in us than we allow ourselves to see, but by our own hearts and heads.

Take responsibility and take off!

The best times are ahead. Now you can start to take on new responsibilities, to take on your *own* responsibilities, and take flight. Just like the butterfly, you have to flap your wings and lift your own weight. Through the struggle you will have gained all the strength you need to spread your own wings and take flight yourself. But you have to be brave, you have to make a move. The only question then is how high do you want to fly?

When a caterpillar morphs into a beautiful butterfly, the world becomes a bigger place. No longer is the bug limited to the few branches that have been its world for so long. Now the sky beckons. Now the new butterfly can roam from shrub to shrub, from tree to tree. When *we* experience positive growth, often our world grows with us.

The direction in which we fly and the altitude to which we climb are totally up to us. Are we content to just cruise through life, or do we want to explore all that the world holds for us? We have to decide. It is true that more adventures bring more dangers. But a butterfly sitting still on a branch is easy prey for a predator. A butterfly in flight is harder to catch.

At the heart of all of our decisions is one common thread: *us*. It is all up to us. We have to take responsibility for our own destiny. Sometimes to get what you deserve, you have to take it. If you want to have what you have always dreamed of, then take responsibility and go get it.

What I've learnt

- Everyone has the ability to change; they just need to be shown how.
- You are not alone in your struggle. There are a lot of people out there who can relate to your pain and fear.
- To change and grow we need a safe environment. This we can create with real friends and a supportive family.
- Once the change has taken place, there will be a time of testing. This provides further opportunities to gain strength.
- We have to take responsibility for our own destiny.

Morphing into top grade material: Craig Stapleton

Craig Stapleton is a rugby league player in the National Rugby League competition in Australia. I have had the privilege of working with him as his personal motivational coach and mentor over the past five years.

When Stapo and I met, he was playing for the St George Illawarra Dragons as a fringe first grade player. He was becoming a dominant force in the reserve grade, or Premier League as it is known, but couldn't quite crack the top grade. He was determined to make his dream of being a dominant first grade footballer and representative player a reality, but he wasn't quite sure how to make it happen. He knew he had the ability, but something seemed to be missing. We had to look at what he was doing and what the current top footballers were doing, and figure out a game plan that would see his career move forward.

Like most players in the NRL, Stapo trained hard. He was a loyal team member and did what the coach asked, but therein lay the problem. That was *all* he was doing. Stapo quickly realised that to get to where he had never been, he had to do what he had never done. He needed extra training, a more disciplined diet, more mental focus, and to think more positively.

Like the true champion he is, Stapo went to work with gusto. At every training session, he put in 100 per cent. All phone conversations contained positive dialogue only. Craig really began to morph into the player he wanted to be and his career started to take off.

The Dragons increased his pay packet, but then he was released amicably so they could sign up some big-name players. So he signed a one-year deal with the

Parramatta Eels, where he became the only forward to play every game that season. He was then invited to go over to England to play Super League for the struggling club Leigh. He excelled there and then returned home to play for the Penrith Panthers. During this time Stapo met and married Jackie and together they are raising five kids.

Stapo wanted to do whatever it took to become a top footballer. He knew it would be a struggle, but he took it on and did the hard work. In the end it was all worth it. He signed a two-year deal with the mighty Cronulla Sharks where he forced his way into the starting line-up and continues to dominate. In 2006 he realised his dream of representing his country when he made the tri-nations training squad and played for Australia against Papua New Guinea.

This man knew he had to change something to get what he wanted and the rewards have been coming ever since. Craig Stapleton morphed himself into one of the most consistent and dominant front row forwards in the toughest rugby league competition in the world, and he's only just begun.

3
Bug, galah, eagle!

Everything that is really great and inspiring
is created by the individual who can labour
in freedom.
Albert Einstein

Freedom of choice

So you want to fly? Where do you want to go? How high
do you want to go? This will depend on your attitude, what
you choose to do. We all have the freedom to choose how
we are going to live, but most of us don't realise what an
incredible gift having this freedom of choice is.

I'd like to explain this freedom to choose by using an
analogy. I want to look at three different levels of flight,
and draw a parallel to three different levels of choice. I'm
going to look at Christmas beetles (bugs), galahs and
eagles. Each have the ability to fly, in much the same way
as we humans have the ability to choose. However, how
they fly is vastly different.

Christmas beetles

Recently I went on a holiday to the Gold Coast in Queensland. At night you would see tens of thousands of Christmas beetles flying around, and the same amount lying all over the ground, on their backs, slowly dying. You see, the Christmas beetle has a strange habit of using its power of flight to destroy itself. Australian Christmas beetles are nocturnal. They come out under the protective cover of night so they won't be seen by predators. But they are attracted to light. So in the safety of night, they fly directly to where they can be seen most clearly of all! Everywhere you see lights – service stations, tennis courts, football fields, parking lots – there they are dying in their thousands. Most of them are destroyed by flying into the lights of oncoming traffic! Their ability to fly becomes their downfall.

There are people who live like this. Their freedom of choice often becomes the very thing that ensnares them. This may be because they have never been taught or shown how to make right decisions. Perhaps they have never had the consequences of bad choices explained to them before they leap to a final decision. Or maybe it's because they harbour bitterness in their hearts, or have been previously badly hurt. For whatever reason, their freedom to choose, sometimes based on a self-opinion of low standing in society, or a position of low self-worth, leads them to make decisions that ultimately hurt

> Where there is lack of vision,
> people perish.
> *Ancient Hebrew proverb*

themselves. Much like the Christmas beetles flying into the lights of the oncoming traffic.

I see this all too often in the juvenile detention centres I work in. I see young people who have so much potential, but instead of using their freedom of choice to find a fulfilling, joyful adventurous life, they choose foolishly, and those decisions land them in lock-up!

This self-destructing way of life can often stem from a lack of vision. 'Where there is lack of vision, people perish' is how the ancient Hebrew saying goes. Lack of vision about how you would like to see yourself or goals you may wish to achieve leads to lack of meaning, lack of drive, lack of passion, lack of hope and a lack of good decision-making ability in your life. This in turn leads to a life lived in fear of making decisions, and as the old saying goes, a life lived in fear, is a life half lived! It is sad, but there are so many people who live life this way. You may have lived your life like this, or perhaps you still are living like this. The great news is, you can change your lack of vision and choose to fly to a higher level.

> A life lived in fear
> is a life half lived.
> *Unknown*

Moving to the next level

How do you see yourself? Is your self-esteem so low that you see yourself as just a bug? Some of us see ourselves as bugs, not because of the bad decisions we have made, but because we have been afraid to make decisions at all. We live our life in fear because we think, 'Who am I to think I can do that?' We see ourself at the bottom of the food chain, nothing but a 'snack' for someone else. However, remember, how we see ourselves is how we will end up.

My favourite movies of all time are the *Rocky* series. Let me draw your attention to a scene in *Rocky V* which demonstrates how if you *see* yourself doing things, you will be able to *do* those things in real life.

In the movie Rocky and his family have returned home to discover their accountant has ripped them off millions of dollars and they find themselves back in the old neighbourhood, scratching for a living. Down and depressed, Rocky visits the old gym where his beloved trainer, Mickey, trained him all those years ago before he passed away.

As Rocky stands in the old dusty gym, he remembers himself shadow sparring and practising. Most of all he remembers Mickey hanging over the ropes ringside yelling encouragingly 'SLIP THE JAB, SLIP THE JAB, see yourself do good, 'cause if you see yourself doin' good, YOU DO GOOD!'

If you want to 'do good' in life, and I presume you do because you're reading this book right now, you need to *see* yourself doing good, and to see yourself as *being* good. How do you see yourself? Perhaps the first thing you need to understand is that you are not a loser, you are not a bug. You are special, beautiful, intelligent, handsome, gorgeous and brilliant!

Most of us, at some time, have seen ourselves as being inadequate and powerless. And this makes us fearful of trying new things, to achieve all we can. But did you know that if you say to yourself, 'I can do this, I can be who I want to be', you are actually helping others to feel the same way? You are actually doing the world a favour! By staying hidden in the corner and saying 'No, I can't do that, I am not good enough' you are not helping yourself and you are definitely not helping anybody else. By letting your true self shine, by aspiring to be as good as you can be, all the time, you are providing an example to everyone around you. And not only that, you are proving your worth to yourself on a daily basis. Just by seeing yourself 'do good' you can increase your self-esteem, start achieving your goals, and encourage and inspire others to do the same. This means that not only you, but everyone you know will all be trying to be the best person they can be, which makes for a pretty happy community!

Galah!

In my analogy, the next level up from a bug is a galah. Now this probably doesn't seem to make much sense at the moment, but bear with me, and I'll use this next story to explain it.

A few years ago I was following my usual early-morning routine of drinking a coffee and gathering my thoughts as I walked around my backyard. There is a wonderful bush corridor behind our house which is a haven for some incredibly beautiful Australian birds. On this particular winter's morning it was really cold. There was ice along the top of the fence and on the children's swings. As the sun rose gently in the east, its warming rays started to thaw the ice, and as the steam rose steadily into the atmosphere, all the birds came to life and took flight from their nesting places. A flock of pink and grey galahs flew overhead.

Have you ever stood and watched a flock of galahs in flight? It is really quite interesting. The birds will be flying along in a straight line, heading towards their destination, wherever that may be, when suddenly, for no apparent reason, one or two birds in the flock will start to zigzag in a sporadic pattern, almost colliding with other members of the flock and sending them spinning out of control to avoid a mid-air accident. And then they just reform and keep on flying. This happens over and over again as you watch them flying off into the distance and seemingly all of the birds have a turn at doing it. They even do it when they are flying on their own. It is really bizarre, and I'm yet to find out why they do it.

As the sun rose in the sky that morning, I also turned my attention to the bugs flying around in the garden that ran along the fence. The bugs didn't fly very high, although they had the same amount of sky to use as the galahs. They just floated and flitted around the garden. They only flew to their ability. Some, like the bees, would venture a little higher, but not much higher. The galahs on the other hand flew higher, faster and swifter than any of the bugs and they seemed to be very determined.

> Attitude is a little thing that
> makes a big difference.
> *Sir Winston Churchill*

Do you want to be a galah?

Even though they had speed, strength and determination, the galahs I observed from my backyard seemed directionless. It was also painfully clear that they were very noisy and disruptive, not only to themselves but also to the others around them. These guys took others out. It is no surprise, then, that the Australian slang for someone who is an idiot or a fool is a 'galah'.

So at this point we can draw a parallel with human behaviour. You may have graduated from the bug class, you may have more belief in yourself now, but what are you doing with your newfound confidence, your speed, and your strength? Have you become a galah?

Some people do become galahs when they develop a belief in themselves. These people are easy to identify. How do I know? That's easy. I was a galah – full of bravado, talented for sure, but directionless and disruptive. Speed? Yep, I had that too, but I was always taking others out.

When galahs realise that they have more strength than they first thought, more speed, more manoeuvrability, more ability, they tend to use these gifts to do

You may have graduated from the bug class ... but have you become a galah?

better work at school, to make more friends, maybe to get a place in a sporting team. But is this all there is to life – a few better grades, more friends, a spot on the school football or netball team?

Galahs are okay if you want to be a noisy pointless parrot making up the numbers in the flock. But ask yourself this: do I just want to be another voice in the crowd? Do I want to hang out with the galahs all my life? If the answer is yes, then great! At least you've taken to the skies, enjoyed the journey and had some fun. You are no longer at the bottom of the food chain, but you might as well put this book down right now, and just enjoy living life in the middle of the road – that's cool! But what if you want to go as far as you can, see all there is to see in life? Do you just want to be heard saying something, or do you want to have something to say?

What if you have a deep yearning to make something of yourself? Well, you have a choice to make. You can choose to stop hanging about with all the other galahs – you can choose to fly to the next level.

If you know deep inside you that you were created for something huge, for something bigger than yourself, if you are hungry for take off, then I dare you to read on.

> When you know what you want,
> and you want it badly enough,
> you will find a way to get it.
> *Jim Rohn*

The eagle

In the introduction I describe my experiences as a sixteen-year-old working on a high-altitude farm in the Kangaroo Valley in New South Wales. I didn't realise it at the time, but I witnessed something during this time that would become a revelation to me over a decade later.

As we unpacked the truck early one morning, I noticed a wedge-tailed eagle soaring directly above us. He was no more than 50 metres above our heads. You could actually see his eyes checking us out. It was truly amazing. He seemed to hover over the worksite, gently drifting from side to side in the breeze.

It was nine in the morning when our new found foreman was joined by his mate. Now there were two of these majestic creatures watching us work. 'This is pretty cool,' I was thinking to myself as we tried to stay focused on the job at hand. The two eagles would hang for hours in the thermal draughts. The fact that neither of these two birds flapped their wings, not once, blew my mind! They were like a pair of gliders hovering in the wind. As you can tell, this picture has stayed in my memory from that day till this. I can see it as vividly as if it happened yesterday.

Do you want to be an eagle? Do you want to reach the heights that this life has to offer? I know I do. I long to see all there is to see for myself and my family. I want to inspire myself, my wife, my children, and countless millions of others to strive for greatness. To be like the eagle, though, means a few changes will have to take place.

> Great spirits have always
> encountered violence
> from mediocre minds.
> *Albert Einstein*

Get ready to change

The eagles I saw were not flying in a flock. In fact eagles never fly in flocks. The eagle is a solitary character. You will only ever see them flying solo or with one other, their mate or sometimes with their children when the chicks are learning to fly. So if you are going to aim to reach your potential and beyond, you need to realise that your flock is going to get thin quite rapidly. There won't be flocks or crowds of people where you're going. Why? Because to reach greatness there will be times of trial, times of adversity, as the saying goes, 'True greatness is born from adversity'. The crowd just won't want to go with you.

And you need to experience adversity on your journey to greatness. I don't know who coined the phrase 'smooth waters never a good sailor will make' but there is much truth in it. If you always get smooth waters, you'll have absolutely no idea what to do or how to handle yourself, or your crew for that matter, let alone the craft you're on, when a storm hits. On the other hand, sailors who have sailed through a storm or two will have the ability to get their boat, their crew and themselves through to sail another day – just ask any sailor who has done more than a couple of Sydney to Hobart yacht races!

> Anyone can hold the helm when the sea is calm.
> *Publilius Syrus*

The point I'm making is this: as you step out to fulfil your dreams, things can and will go wrong. That's just a fact of life. Life revolves around human beings co-existing together in a less than perfect world. Within the framework of society, they have to relate to each other while trying to achieve both personal and corporate goals which may be based on different belief systems of individuals and groups with different agendas and ideals. Whew!!

So, stuff is going to go wrong! However, taking into account the fact that we can learn from our own experiences and the experiences of others, and if we are wise and determined not to make those same mistakes again, we should be able to minimise the number of negative experiences we go through.

Having said that, seeing your dreams come to pass can be easier said than done. If fulfilling a dream was

> You don't become enormously successful
> without encountering and overcoming a
> number of extremely challenging problems.
> *Mark Victor Hansen*

easy, everybody would be doing it. But it is hard work, and yes even the best make mistakes, Michael Jordan didn't always land the perfect three-point bomb right at the buzzer to win the game for his team. Tiger Woods doesn't always land on the fairway, Roger Federer does tend to frame the ball from time to time, and James Packer and Lachlan Murdoch did make some mistakes with One.Tel.

Ladies and gentlemen, boys and girls, mistakes happen! Some can be painful, some can be costly, in the case of One.Tel $1 billion costly! But James Packer is back, stronger, wiser and richer than ever. Now there's a good sailor. But there are few who are willing to go to the other side of the lake for fear of the storm that may come. That's why eagles fly alone or only in the company of a few. However it's only through the storm that you get your sea legs, your strength.

Let's look at the eagle again for a minute. The eagle can fly higher than most other birds, except perhaps vultures. He can see further and fly faster than most. He is without peer as predator in the bird world – he is at the top of the food chain. He is free to fly where he wants. If you go through the tough times of growth you will find that the rewards are definitely worth it. One day you too will be able to use your freedom just like the eagle, and soar.

The choice is yours

So I ask you again, who do you want to be? Do you want to remain a bug, dodging for cover, always on the lookout for predators, barely getting by? Or are you happy to hang with the galahs, going along just to get along but with no real purpose or sense of destiny, where there is safety in numbers but where you will get knocked around from time to time, where you might do okay, but never better than the average? Or do you want to make the most of your ability and take to the sky? Do you want to take on the challenges, soar to the highest heights, fulfil your dream, enjoy the view?

> **Life is too short to live a life full of regret. Live a passionate life, a life of adventure.**

So what will you be? A bug, a galah or an eagle? The choice is yours and yours alone. There are no excuses. Excuses are like armpits – everybody has a couple and they both stink! Life is too short to live a life full of regret. Live a passionate life, a life of adventure.

One example of a person living a passionate life is Jesse Martin. Jesse was seventeen years old when he became the youngest person to sail solo around the world. One night on his epic adventure when he was passing through the world's most treacherous ocean just south of Cape Horn in Argentina, his boat rolled over four times. A rollover is where a boat is smashed by waves and turned upside down and then rights itself. One was common, but it happened to Jesse four times in that one night! The water was like ice, and he was frightened, cold, hungry and alone. The on-board camera filmed him crying and saying, 'I want to go home, I hate this ...'

After watching this footage with Jesse, a TV interviewer asked him, 'Did you think you were going to die? Wouldn't that have been a tragedy?'

Jesse answered him with words that fuelled something inside me that was already aflame. 'Yes I thought I was going to die, but that wouldn't have been a tragedy.' With tears in his eyes now, he continued, 'A tragedy is a man who lives till he is about 90 and never fulfils his dream. I was seventeen, and I would have died living my dream!'

Jesse Martin is an eagle! *And you can be too!*

When I sit back and take a good hard look at life and what it has to offer, the choice, for me, is easy: I want the thermals, thanks! How about you? What's your dream?

What I've learnt

- Once you have chosen to change, you must decide which level you want to fly to: bug, galah or eagle.
- Freedom of choice is a gift that needs to be used wisely.
- To reach your potential there will have to be sacrifices.
- The higher you fly, the better the view.
- At the end of the day the choice is yours. Believe in yourself and your own potential. You *can* soar like an eagle.

Taking to the skies: Leo

Sixteen-year-old Leo lived in a low socio-economic area. He had wonderful supportive parents, but didn't see much for himself or his future, his opinion of himself was pretty low. He didn't see his worth and therefore didn't think he was worth anything. Leo had a dream, but thought that it would only ever stay in his imagination.

Leo went on a DARE:Ops camp after his best mate Jamie came back from one and just wouldn't shut up about it. Jamie told Leo how he had learned that he had so much more potential than he had ever realised. He kept on saying that Leo just had to go on a camp until eventually Leo turned up for selection to our next camp. He proved to be one of the most enthusiastic participants we have ever had. Leo learned not only to fly higher than the bugs but that he could soar like an eagle. He learnt that he *is* worth his dream and that he can make it become a reality.

Leo returned home from the camp and began to express his love for his family in positive ways that astounded his parents. They were utterly amazed at the way Leo's perspective on life had altered. It changed dramatically when he realised that how high he flew wasn't determined by his postcode or his bank balance but rather by his thoughts and attitudes, and ultimately what he does with them.

Leo is one of the guys who truly lives what he has learnt. He has gone on to become one of our most trusted and reliable peer leaders, volunteering as a leader at other camps. He has secured a job at a local ex-servicemen's club where the board absolutely love him. He has represented my organisation at several high profile business meetings and is well on his way to soaring among the eagles. Leo no longer allows his environment to dictate his future. He has learnt that he has the power to choose his own destiny and his own altitude. His dream is to own a purple Kenworth prime mover and be a truck driver just like his dad, and now he believed he can actually do it. Leo is taking to the skies!

4
Teamwork makes the dream work

Keep away from people who try to belittle
your ambitions.
Small people always do that,
but the really great ones make you feel that
you, too, can become great.
Mark Twain

Where to from here?

In this chapter I want to explore where we go from here.
We have just discussed how the level at which you want
to fly in life is determined by the decisions you make, as
well as by the people you hang around and associate
with. Although you may aim to be an eagle, understanding
that there will only be few who will fly with you is
important. It is also important to understand that even
eagles cannot survive and be productive on their own. It
takes two eagles to produce a family and feed them, raise
them, teach them how to fly.

Consequently, you will need to develop relationships
and partnerships with the right people to see your dreams

come to fruition. In other words, you need to build the right team to see your dreams succeed.

The value of relationships

We all need strong, healthy relationships in our lives. We need to have people around us whom we love and value. They in turn will love and value us. They will care for us and build us up, not bring us down. People like this want us to be free to realise our potential, and they will put your needs before their own.

Some relationships, on the other hand, can be very destructive. A destructive relationship is one that takes away your freedom to choose for yourself. You may feel trapped, and like you can't make a move without permission. This may be caused by fear of violent reprisal if you don't do what you are told. Or you may have experienced emotional manipulation by a person who lets you know they will be hurt if you say this or do that, and holds you almost solely responsible for their emotional well-being. If you are in one of these relationships, get out of it or it will destroy you!

> A real friend is someone who walks in when the rest of the world walks out.
> *Unknown*

There are some people I don't hang around with any more, simply because life has taken us in different directions. Then there are others I never want to see again because they don't encourage my dreams and let me be my true self. And there are those in my life right now whom I love and value. I have learned the value of strong, healthy relationships. How did I learn that you might ask? Hmm … I'm going to get a little personal here, so please bear with me.

A bad relationship

When I was eighteen, a guy I worked with introduced me to a group of people who at first seemed really nice. They were friendly and seemed to be pretty smart. I got involved with them mainly because I wanted to feel accepted. We'd all hang out together, go to dinner, that sort of stuff. All pretty innocent really, for the first few months anyway. Eventually I moved in with a couple of the guys from the group.

These people received my trust and respect, but then they started using that to influence my decision making. They made me believe that if I didn't hang with them my life would fall apart because I was nothing without them. They told me I was selfish and immature to follow my silly little goals, and called me a 'dreamer'. They said I was full of selfish ambition, and only interested in building my own kingdom. The relationship got so clouded and confusing that at one point I lost any sense of self-worth, any sense of individual identity. I valued these people's opinions so much over my own that I remained involved with them for the next eight years. I felt trapped!

Co-dependency occurs when two people need each other in order to feel value and worth; without each other they both feel worthless. And I, you see, had allowed myself to get sucked into a group of co-dependent people. These people made me feel valuable and wanted, simply by telling me that I had certain needs and problems and that they could *help* me and indeed *wanted* to help me with. When someone wants to help you, you automatically feel valued. In turn, the helper gets *their* feeling of importance by offering to help.

Co-dependent people fit into one of two categories: the victim or the rescuer. The rescuer is the one who manipulates the victim by sayings things like, 'If you leave me, no-one else will help you and you will be alone and maybe even die!' The victim can manipulate the rescuer too, saying things like, 'If you don't help me I'll die, and it will be your fault.' It is weird I know, but many of us live like this, even within our own families.

> No man is good enough to govern
> another man without that other's consent.
> *Abraham Lincoln*

Luckily, I eventually broke free from the group. I was fortunate enough to maintain some healthy relationships with people outside the group. The voice of these positive friends, along with the voice of my heart, soon showed me that the relationships I had with these people was not helping me grow and fulfil my potential. In fact, I was actually doing the opposite!

I ended the relationships by building on the positive friendships I did have, and gradually starving the negative relationships. It only makes sense that what you feed in your life will flourish, and what you starve will die, and so, over time, the negative relationships disappeared altogether.

> A successful person is one
> who can lay a firm foundation
> with the bricks that others throw at them.
> *David Brink*

Learning from it

I learned three incredibly valuable lessons in that period of my life which have helped me become the man I am today. The first lesson I learned was how *not* to treat people. The second was to keep following my own dreams. And the third valuable lesson was to continue building relationships with people outside my immediate circle of life, who would teach me how to fish rather than feed me fish on a regular basis, to keep me dependent on them.

I have now ended all relationships that I have identified as co-dependent. The relationships I value today are inter-dependent. I look for relationships with people who can add to my feeling of self-worth but who don't do it out of a need to feel valued – they are secure in themselves. I, in turn, can make these people feel more valued, and I don't need to get my sense of self-worth from doing that. We just enjoy being friends. We are all partners, heading in the same direction with like-minded passions, our own dreams to fulfil, encouraging each other along the way.

There is great value in positive healthy relationships. Good people can help you go a long way. Value the people who push you to succeed for your sake, not for theirs. They are worth far more than you realise. They make valuable members of your team and will help you achieve your dreams.

The power of teamwork

Who you have as members on your team is extremely important as the power of teamwork is incredible. There is nothing like watching a well-trained, well-disciplined team in action, such as the World Cup soccer team, an international cricket team or an Olympic-standard hockey team. Another example of a world-class team are the crack Australian SAS soldiers. Even when they are vastly outnumbered in the field, they are extremely effective. These guys are regarded as the second-best trained soldiers in the world; only the Israeli Special Forces are considered their peers.

Why are they so good? Because they all work together as a single unit! Each member of a five-man team has a special function and every role is respected by everyone in the team. A very good mate of mine used to serve in the Australian SAS unit. He told me the reason the guys are so good is that they train continually, and that everyone watches out for their mates' best interests because they know that everyone has something to offer the team. These fellas really live the slogan:

T ogether
E veryone
A chieves
M ore

I think of life as a sport sometimes. That probably comes from my intense involvement in sport as a youngster, and even as a senior athlete. In sport, especially team sports, if everyone had the same selfish mentality on the field as they do in personal life or business, what would happen? Take the game of rugby, for example. What would happen if the team had a forward pack that didn't want to run with the ball, or even just one forward who didn't like getting tackled? Or what if you had a fly-half who never passed the ball but hogged it all the time? What if your wingers and centres weren't disciplined enough to stay in their own positions but came looking for the ball instead of waiting for it? What would happen? You'd get smashed by your opposition every time!

> Help others achieve their dreams
> and you will achieve yours.
> *Les Brown*

A team works by giving. The winger can't score if the fly-half won't pass the ball. The fly-half can't get the ball unless the forwards are willing to do the hard yards up the middle. Your team can't win unless you stop the other team from scoring, and that means everyone has to work hard at defence, putting their bodies on the line. Teamwork makes the dream work!

That's why it is so important to surround yourself with good people. When I won the NSW state boxing title in 1998, I had to fight all of the bouts myself, that is true. But it was a team of trainers, coaching staff, sports psychologists, sparring partners and a supportive family that helped make my dream come true. Without the support and teamwork of all of those people, I wouldn't have won. Building, connecting, partnering together, thinking of others just as much as yourself, it all adds up to a recipe to achieve your chosen dream. It also helps you have a great life!

Only yoking!

As I talked about in Chapter 3, making decisions about how to live our lives can be influenced by our emotions. Our emotions are influenced by the people we choose to have around us and as members of our teams. So it's really important to make sure we choose our team-mates carefully. We need to hook up with the right people in order to make our dreams a reality.

Do you know what an old fashioned yoke was? It was a piece of farming equipment that was placed across the shoulders of two huge oxen. Chains would be attached from the yoke to a plough behind the oxen. To choose the most effective team to plough his fields, good old Farmer Joe would have to pair his oxen according to their size and strength for the most effective team. So he had to be careful which two oxen he partnered together. The same applies to us as we move towards fulfilling our dreams. We have to be careful who we choose as our partners and who we build relationships with in order to achieve our dreams.

> The more you seek security, the less of it you have. But the more you seek opportunity, the more likely it is that you will achieve the security you desire.
> *Brian Tracey*

There are plenty of people who are just waiting for someone with a dream to come along so they can attach themselves to it. Let me tell you about one such person I met.

I'll call this guy Fred to hide his true identity. Fred always wanted to know what ideas I was working on or what new idea I had. I noticed that every time I shared an idea with him, he would always put his spin on it, and told me how it could be done differently. Oh, and best of all, he always told me what percentage cut he would take! He was pretty bold about it as well. He wouldn't go away and think about it and try to change your mind over time. No, this bloke Fred, he'd just say it to your face. Gotta give him credit, he had guts and wasn't afraid of offending anyone, as long as it made him money. I observed him actually formulating partnerships with people and the results were always the same. Time and again the dream would be dragged off course and the partnership would go nowhere. Each and every time you would hear how Fred had all these great ideas and took the partnership in the wrong direction and it all eventually fell in a heap.

Sometimes we just 'hook up' with people so we get approval

You don't want to be yoked with people like Fred. If Farmer Joe put a taller, stronger ox with a smaller, weaker and slower ox, what do you think would happen? The poor old farmer would have a hell of a time trying to keep the plough straight. He would spend so much time and energy trying to simply stay on course that he would actually make very little forward motion. Sometimes we just 'hook up' with people so we get approval, so we feel validated and accepted. In the end, however, this type of partner will slow you down, or stop you completely.

Weaker beasts

If you get partnered with someone like Fred (I call them weaker beasts), they will slow you down and pull you off course. Remember you are the stronger of the two in this equation. You have all the ideas. You have the dream and the passion to drive it. Don't let the weaker beast slow you down and pull you off track so that you make very little forward progress. At the end of the day, the weaker beast knows that there will always be another ox to hook up with. Together you might just end up going to the slaughterhouse!

> All men of action are dreamers.
> *James G Huneker*

Parallel partners

Just as there are 'weaker beasts', there are also people I call 'parallel partners'. These types of people think like men of action and act like men of thought. If you choose to yoke yourself with people like this, you stay on course. You tend to achieve more in a shorter space of time, and take far less energy to do it. The following story from Texas shows how parallel partnerships can help, not hinder, you.

There used to be a huge annual rodeo festival in Texas where one of the main attractions was the draughthorse pull. Farmers from all over the countryside would enter their best draughthorse in the competition to see which was the strongest animal. The horse would be fastened to a sled without wheels which was loaded with bags of flour or wheat and made to pull it.

One year the winner pulled 5 tonnes. The horse that came second pulled about 4 tonnes. The organisers then wondered what would happen if they yoked the two horses together, expecting them to pull about 10 tonnes. So the two draughthorses were both yoked to a sled which had 10 tonnes of bags on it. To the crowd's amazement, the horses seemed to use little effort to drag the sled. So more and more bags were piled on until the horses could not move the sled any more. Before they were stymied by the weight of the bags, the two most powerful horses together pulled almost 30 tonnes, more than three times the weight of their individual efforts combined.

Connecting, not networking!

I've noticed the buzzword 'networking' being used in the motivational speaking world, and even more so in the corporate world! I don't really dig that term, for the simple reason that everyone I have seen 'networking' appears to be looking for people to help them get a leg up, a free lunch. That selfish mentality comes through again and again. Me, me, me, me. 'Let's form a network!' they'll say when what they really mean is 'Where can *you* take *me* from here and where do I drop you off?'

> In the long run, we shape our lives
> and we shape ourselves.
> The process never ends. And the choices
> we make are ultimately our own responsibility.
> *Eleanor Roosevelt*

I said earlier that I value solid, healthy relationships. This includes business relationships as well. I think that the best and safest way to do business is for individuals to treat each other with respect, honour and dignity. But sadly that is not always the way people in business treat each other. Now I know some business people network for the common good. So let me clarify where I am coming from. It is on a more personal level, where individuals treat each other as businesses and not as individuals, that I get ticked off. I see people networking with each other with what I call a 'ladder' mentality. It's almost as if they are thinking, 'I'll just use you as another rung on my ladder to see how high you can take me. Once I'm there, I'll just keep moving up and, well, who cares what happens to you?'

Some say that's business. I say that sucks!

I like to connect with people. I try to form positive relationships that build good things for both parties, to create a platform from which everyone can benefit. Doing things this way can cause you to miss out on opportunities that will prop you up in the short term, but it will not build you into a person with integrity and honour. Connecting with others on a foundation of respect and integrity can help you build solid relationships that transcend business, and can actually help you meet people who will become life-long friends as well. Now who doesn't need good friends, eh?

> The greatest discovery of my generation
> is that human beings can alter their
> lives by altering their attitudes of mind.
> *James Allen*

SOS!

Friends are what help us fulfil our potential and make our lives more rewarding and rich. True friends are ones who will often put their needs before theirs. Unfortunately many people in our communities do not reflect this attitude towards each other. I have called this section 'SOS' for a reason. In Morse code SOS stands for 'Save Our Souls'. Now there is team mentality: there is no 'my' or 'I' in that message. It's an 'us/our' message. However

I am going to take the liberty of using the letters SOS to show something a little different. I'm going to use these letters to ask a question. It's a question I think we all need to consider because not doing so could be the undoing of our dream.

Here is the question: 'Are you **S**tupid **O**r **S**elfish?'

Let's face it; we've all done something stupid in our lives, some of us more than our fair share. We've all done dumb things, stuff we're ashamed of or embarrassed about. I know I have! Many of us do stupid things all the time and don't even know we're doing them. This is why if we don't ask ourselves the question, we could bring ourselves undone.

> We must learn to live together as brothers
> or perish together as fools.
> *Martin Luther King*

Working on building-sites in the construction industry was a real eye-opener for me. It showed me how many people do many stupid things and just don't see it. On a building-site there are tradesmen from several different trades, their labourers, the site labourers, supervising staff and sub-contractors all trying to work together for a common goal – to get the building up and finished as quickly as possible. The faster the construction, the larger the profit! Now commonsense says that each tradesman would want to cooperate with the other tradesmen to make the job faster and easier. But commonsense isn't that common!

The worst attributes of the human character come out whenever greed is involved. On one building-site I worked on tools would go missing, especially when a particular group of men were on the site. This would slow down the other tradesmen because they would have to spend valuable time either looking for the tools or going to the hardware suppliers to buy more. This caused a feeling of distrust to spread throughout the whole site. People began saying things behind each other's backs and a feeling of disharmony spread like cancer. Tradesmen started the day's work already stressed because the job was going slower than they had thought it would, and therefore they weren't going to make the profit they had counted on. All because of someone's stupid decision not to return the tools. When someone does something stupid, you can bet your bottom dollar it was because of a selfish motive. People who do stupid things are often only thinking of themselves. Some of the worst drivers you see on the road are more often than not acting selfishly. Here's a perfect example of everyday stupid behaviour stemming from selfishness.

The parking lot

I was leaving the local shopping mall when I witnessed some astonishingly selfish driving, just in the car park! The place was packed – it was two days before Christmas. A bloke was waiting patiently for me to reverse out of my spot so he could park there. Then this other driver tried to push his way between me and the guy waiting, as I was reversing out! He got himself jammed between the two of us, so I couldn't get out and the guy waiting patiently couldn't get in, plus a whole heap of other stressed-out pre-Christmas shoppers in their cars were blocked as well.

Mr Impatience eventually pushed passed us, but if he had just waited 45 seconds or so, he would have had been able to pass easily, I would have been happily heading down the exit ramp, and the other drivers wouldn't have been held up. Instead he caused a lot of people to become pretty flustered and created a rather unpleasant ordeal that took quite a few minutes to sort out. Stupid! Or just selfish?

Have a look at your own life. If you are honest with yourself, I bet you'll find some of your biggest mistakes were made when you thought you were thinking of others but really you were thinking of what the benefits for you might be! How it would make you look, how it would make you feel, what you could get out of it, how you would benefit. C'mon, be honest. If you are honest with yourself, you can be honest with others.

Realising that we do stupid things because of selfishness is the key to not doing stupid things! If we can train ourselves to think of others as well as ourselves, we will end up making much wiser decisions. Stupid things will be something of the past. Dreams are strengthened through wisdom; they are weakened through selfishness.

What I've learnt

- Getting caught up in the wrong type of relationship can be very destructive. Having positive, healthy relationships is very powerful.
- Make a point to learn from the things you experience in life – positives can always come from negatives.
- Teams can achieve more than individuals.
- Commonsense is not that common.
- Stupidity can often arise from a selfish attitude that is put into action.

Teamwork in action: Dara Torres

Dara Torres is an American swimmer who first competed in the Olympics in Los Angeles in 1984 where she won a gold medal in the 4 × 100-metre freestyle. She then went on to compete in the next three Olympics, winning gold in Seoul in 1988, gold in Barcelona in 1992 and three bronze medals in Sydney in 2000. Dara then retired and decided to have a baby. But retirement only held her interest for so long. Now, at the grand old age of 40, she is preparing to make a comeback at the Beijing Olympics in 2008. If she makes the American Olympic team, she will be the oldest female swimmer to compete at this, the highest, level.

But Dara is not doing it alone. She is the perfect example of 'teamwork makes the dream work'. Her support team consists of many people, each with a specific role. Steve Sierra and Anne Tierney are her trainers and massage therapists. These two put Dara through gruelling stretching regimes several times a week, with each session lasting two hours. Stretching is vital to maintain Dara's suppleness, so she can keep up with her much younger competitors. After every training session or race, Dara also receives an intense massage to help prevent injury.

David Hoffman is Dara's partner and a key member of Dara's support crew. Not only does he play Mr Mum with their fourteen-month-old daughter, Tessa, while Dara is training and competing, he also supports Dara emotionally in her efforts to make the US swimming team.

Then there is Dara's head coach, Michael Lohberg, who plans and oversees the type of training Dara has to do in order for this amazing dream to become a reality.

Her sprint coach, Chris Jackson, helps Dara focus on her technique and make the most of every last particle of her energy so she can achieve maximum output when it counts. Last but not least is strength and conditioning coach, Andy O'Brien. Andy helps build Dara's strength making sure she doesn't bulk up too much, so that she is strong but sleek in the water.

And we mustn't forget Dara herself. This mother-of-one's motivation and desire to win is what fuels each member of her support crew. Dara explains that her motivation to race is due to the fact that she is 'so freaking competitive it's unbelievable'. But she knows that she can't make a successful comeback to the elite level of swimming without her team. She knows that 'teamwork makes the dream work'!

5
The gondola

A decision is made with the brain. A commitment
is made with the heart. Therefore, a commitment is
much deeper and more binding than a decision.

Nido Qubein

A solid base

I like to draw analogies between life and objects that
seem to have very little to do with what I'm talking
about. Take, for example, a hot-air balloon. A hot-air
balloon seemingly has nothing to do with our life or our
dreams. Well, let me show you what we can learn from a
simple hot-air balloon.

To draw an analogy between our life and a hot-air
balloon, we need to break it down, piece by piece. Over
the next few chapters we will take a look at the vital
components that make a hot-air balloon take to the sky
and fly freely and safely. By comparing ourselves with

the balloon, we will be able to see what we need in our lives to help us make our dreams become a reality.

What is the first thing we would need to make a hot-air balloon functional? Let's start with the base. You have to have a solid base and the base of a hot-air balloon is the basket, known as the gondola. The gondola is very important as it carries the cargo and what a precious cargo – it carries people! In this analogy the gondola represents your base, and your base is you, your character and those who support you at home. I thank God for the support of my wife and children. Without their support through the tough times, our dreams would never have materialised. Sure we could have flown to a great height, but if the gondola was rotten or weak, we could also have fallen from a great height!

> **Character is what you would do if no-one was looking, and no-one would find out!**

> Only a man's character is the
> real criterion of worth.
> *Eleanor Roosevelt*

I've heard character described this way: 'Character is what you would do if no-one was looking, and no-one would find out!' Hmm, interesting! What is your character like? Only you can answer that, but let me ask you this: If your gondola was made of poor-quality material, what do you think could happen? Or what if your gondola was not well maintained, poorly looked after? There may be a build-up of small splits and cracks in the walls and flooring; perhaps the stitching is waterlogged, causing rot to form in the binds. What could happen if you took off in that balloon and climbed to a height of 2000 metres? The potential for disaster is obvious. The flooring could give way and disaster would surely strike. It's the same with the way you live your life, how you 'do' life. The quality of your gondola, your base, will decide whether you will succeed in making your dreams become realities.

What kind of person are you?

Building your base, your character, with the right material is of great importance. This is what will sustain you and keep you safe when your dream takes off.

So, what condition is your base in? What are you made of? To answer this, you need to think about the following questions:

- Are you a person with integrity?
- Are you honest or are you a liar?
- Is your word your bond?
- Does your 'yes' mean 'yes' and your 'no' mean 'no'?
- Do you say what you mean and mean what you say?
- Can people rely on you or are you unreliable?
- Do you try to manipulate and control people?
- What kind of person are you?

> Small opportunities are often the beginning of great enterprises.
> *Demosthenes*

It looks good, but does it work?

Building your gondola with the right materials is certainly of great importance, but how will you know it works? At some point you will have to test your character to find out. My character was tested when I led an expedition across the second-hardest trek in the world, the legendary Kokoda Track in Papua New Guinea.

I'll take your ten worst students to a real war zone. I'll take them to the Kokoda Track, and I'm paying!

On 3 October 2003 I read an article in a national newspaper branding a certain school a 'war zone'. I felt it was unfair that a whole school was branded a war zone because of the action of one former student. So I did what anyone passionate about something does – I jumped in without thinking. I rang the school and offered to get them some positive press to counteract the negative stuff they had been hammered with. I said, 'I'll take your ten worst students to a real war zone. I'll take them to the Kokoda Track, and I'm paying!'

I should add here that at this point I only knew of the Kokoda Track because my grandfather had fought there in the Second World War. He had shared many wartime stories with my brother Craig and I when we were growing up. I'd never been to Kokoda and had never met anyone who had, besides my grandfather. I didn't know how to get there or who would take me. I knew nothing of the costs involved, the culture of the local people, the insurance required, the team needed to look after these kids or what the safety protocols were! Nothing, I knew nothing!

> Leadership is the challenge to be something
> more than average.
> *Jim Rohn*

Still, I couldn't sit back and let the media slam all of the students in this school because of the actions of a few. The high school *was* a violent place, that I must say. On my first visit there, a week after my phone call, I was confronted by an administration office that had a security code keypad on the entrance door to keep staff safe and students *out*. I also saw a teacher who had been attacked physically by students that day and was bruised and bleeding. Another teacher was suffering from a nervous breakdown because his students had rioted in his second-storey classroom. They had thrown his desk down two flights of stairs, smashed the windows, and then proceeded to throw the classroom chairs out of the broken windows. To say the school was rough was an understatement.

> You have two hands, one to help yourself.
> The second to help others.
> *Anonymous*

After I had met the principal and the staff in the staff common room, I again laid down the challenge: 'How would you like some positive press? I can get it for you, I'll take your ten worst students to a real war zone and I'm paying!'

The staff all jumped enthusiastically at the opportunity. There were many questions such as: 'Can you really do this?', 'Are you sure?', 'Is it safe?', 'What will it cost us?' And of course there were a few saying 'The parents will never support this!'

Do you remember the question 'Do you say what you mean and mean what you say?' Well, I do mean what I say but had I known what was involved to pull this dream off, I would probably never have offered. Sometimes ignorance is bliss! However, I was committed now. For me there was no option: this had to be done.

> People of mediocre ability sometimes achieve outstanding success because they don't know when to quit. Most men succeed because they are determined to.
>
> *George E Allen*

Pulling it off

I had given my word to the school so now I had to do what I had said I would do. Although the Kokoda is the second-hardest trek on the planet, walking it was the easy part! Organising the trip, raising the funds and arranging for a film crew to cover the expedition and get it to air, now that was hard! I located the legendary Charlie Lynn, arguably the world's foremost expert on the track and its history, and he agreed to lead us. Once I had organised my team and started to pull the whole thing together, I had the daunting task of trying to raise the funds for this project. After all, I had said I'd pay. Making a long story short, I was able to raise over $150 000. This covered all the

Although the Kokoda is the second-hardest trek on the planet, walking it was the easy part!

costs such as airfares, accommodation, backpacks, food, insurance, clothing, the whole box and dice.

> Only a life lived for others is a life worthwhile.
> *Albert Einstein*

The building materials that made up my gondola held up under all the weight of expectation and pressure. And, believe me, there was incredible pressure! But I was able to pull it off. It would have been so much easier to back out once I realised what was involved, but I had integrity, I had to go forward. To go back on my word was not an option, and the reward, well, it far outweighed the sacrifice.

The young men we took on the track went home and helped the staff at the school to reduce the rate of violence by over 70 per cent in the following twelve months. The story of the trip was aired on television and the positive coverage we received from magazines, radio, newspapers and television was sensational.

> All glory comes from daring to begin.
> *Eugene F Ware*

Maintaining the gondola

As a consequence of that trip, I was offered my own television series. I thought that I'd made it! However this is where I almost came totally undone. I got a big head.

The TV series went to air in April 2006 and won the ratings for its timeslot by only the second episode. I thought I had it made in the shade! I was certain that schools would begin beating a path to my door to have me, a TV star, speak to their students. Meanwhile I organised another extreme trip, this time to Western Samoa, with nine troubled young men, two teachers and a police officer. We left for the trip on the same day that the final episode went to air, and I assumed I'd come back to a mass of email invitations and more work than I could poke a stick at.

> Pride goes before destruction,
> and a haughty spirit before a fall.
> *Ancient Hebrew proverb*

WRONG! I came back to three months of nothing. No work, no money, nothing. I had to humble myself, stop believing my own press and get out there and keep doing what I knew best. I had to get back to basics, work hard, never give up, and continue to work on my character. You can't get caught up with how good your gondola looks. You have to make sure it is built to last, to withstand the pressure that life brings. You can do that by staying grounded and humble. Sure, enjoy your success, but don't let it go to your head.

I thought that getting a big head would never happen to me, but it did, and it almost cost me everything.

I thought that getting a big head would never happen to me, but it did, and it almost cost me everything. Your family can only go without food for so long, and your marriage can withstand only so much pressure. Stay focused on the things that matter, and then the things that don't won't cloud your judgement.

What I've learnt

- Without a solid base, disaster is only a flight away.
- Taking action is what gets things done.
- The materials with which you build the foundation of your life can support you or destroy you. The choice is yours so build wisely.
- Never believe your own press. Stay humble or you will be humiliated.

The power of a strong gondola: Evander Holyfield

On Monday, 30 June 1997, the world was in shock as the story of one of the most cowardly and outwardly insane events in the sporting world unfolded in newspapers and on televisions across the globe. Evander Holyfield, the people's champion, had beaten 'Iron' Mike Tyson for the second time to retain his heavyweight boxing crown. But the fashion in which the fight was conducted was one of the most preposterous in history.

It was obvious from the outset that Tyson's favourite weapon, intimidation, was having no effect on Holyfield after the beating Holyfield had inflicted on Tyson in their previous meeting. In that fight Evander the 'Real Deal' Holyfield had knocked out 'Iron' Mike Tyson in the eleventh round in emphatic style. On June 30, Holyfield took the fight to Tyson in the first rounds; there was no running or backing away. Tyson threw his best at the champion who showed no signs of slowing down, but just kept coming. By the third round Holyfield's superior athleticism and boxing prowess were obvious.

Tyson attempted to start the third round without his mouthpiece but was ordered to put it in. He obeyed referee Miles Lane but quickly spat it out again as the round got under way. Tyson got Holyfield in a clinch and bit off a huge chunk of his right ear! When the referee realised Holyfield was missing part of his ear, he warned Tyson not to bite, but when the fight was resumed, Tyson grabbed Holyfield in another clinch and bit his left ear, doing enough damage to send the champion to hospital for plastic surgery.

The man who had become the youngest ever heavyweight champion of the world in 1986 at just 21 years of age, the man who had dominated the world boxing ranks until 1990 when he suffered his first defeat at the hands of James 'Buster' Douglas, had just shown the world what he was truly made of. Mike Tyson had all the talent in the world, but his character was left wanting.

Talent can take you to the top, but character keeps you there. Holyfield has become an icon in the sport and is recognised as a true champion in and out of the ring with his acts of generosity, church and community involvement and his positive lifestyle. Evander Holyfield's dream is to become the first man in history to win the world heavyweight title five times. He has already won four, thus breaking the record set by the great Muhammad Ali. Holyfield's character, his gondola, has remained strong in the face of adversity, keeping him at the top of his game, and his life.

Tyson, on the other hand, has been charged with numerous offences from drink driving, road rage and possession of drugs to assault and rape, for which he served three years in gaol. On top of that, he has been through many broken relationships and has lost hundreds of millions of the dollars that his talent in the ring earned him. 'Iron' Mike Tyson's character clearly isn't made of iron. It is sad to see what can happen to someone if their gondola isn't strong enough to support their dream. But Mike Tyson is still learning. I truly hope that he will build and maintain his character to a level befitting a champion. Just like the legendary Evander Holyfield who has proven himself to be the 'Real Deal'!

SO... WHAT'S WITH THE NEGATIVITY? CAN'T A GUY HAVE A DREAM?
WE TOTALLY SUPPORT YOU DUDE! IT'S JUST THAT IT'S REALLY HARD TO WIN MISS UNIVERSE!
HAHAHA!!
HEE HEE HEE
HA HA
Hoo Hoo Hoo

6
The canopy

All that we are is the result
of what we have thought.
Buddha

What is a dream?

We have established the first part of the hot-air balloon
analogy: the gondola or basket represents our base. The
strength of our base depends on our character and how
we live our lives. Now comes the next vital component of
a hot-air balloon, the canopy.

The canopy holds the air that makes the balloon
float. In this analogy, the canopy represents your dream.
The canopy needs to be strong and sturdy: there should
be no frayed stitching or holes. Do you have a dream? Are
there any holes in it? Imagine the questions a possible
financial backer of your dream might ask you. That'll
soon show you if there are any holes.

What is a dream anyway? The dictionary defines a dream as an ambition, or as something that you long for, hope for. Do you have an 'ambition'? Do you long for something? What do you hope you can achieve? Remember, this is a book to help you be the best you want to be!

> Dreams are pure thought,
> An opportunity to discover yourself.
> *Joe Brown*

When I was fifteen or sixteen I couldn't really articulate what my dream was. I don't think I could do it at age twenty for that matter. So how do you know what your dream is? Let's take one step back; let's find out what you are passionate about. When you identify that, you will be well on your way to discovering your dream. So take a few moments right now to identify what you are passionate about.

Is there a difference between what we are passionate about and our dreams? Yes, there certainly is. My passion is youth: to communicate to them the possibilities and opportunities open to them, to see them live a fulfilled life while encouraging others around them to do the same. My dream is to become the greatest youth communicator on the planet, ever, in the history of the world.

Let's take another example. I'm very passionate about my wife and kids; I love them insatiably. My dream for my family is to see them want for nothing, to see them all become the best at whatever they choose to do with their life. The difference between passion and dream is that passion is the intangible, the irrational, the motivating force, whereas a dream is the real goal, 'the stuff' you want to do or have. It's the result of your passion.

So where do our dreams come from? What makes our mind see things that don't exist in the present but which we believe could become real in the future? I believe our dreams are born from experiences we have had: events we have witnessed, stories we have heard, what we watch on television, what music we listen to. All these experiences influence our imagination and, as a consequence, what dreams we develop.

> Imagination is everything.
> It is the preview of life's coming attractions.
> *Albert Einstein*

Choosing to dream

Why do we dream of doing things or having stuff? I believe it is human nature to want to be great, to be positive, to achieve, and I think having dreams inspires us to be great. Here's a tip, though: if we don't make the choice to go after our dream and turn it into something real, it will only ever be a dream. Remember the galahs? It is all too easy to be distracted from pursuing our dream, to knock around with the crowd, living life with a 'peace at any price' mentality.

> The future belongs to those who
> believe in the beauty of their dreams.
> *Eleanor Roosevelt*

Are we worth the dream?

One of the most influential factors affecting whether we dream or not is our self-esteem, what we believe we are worth. If we believe we are worth an amazing career, then we will believe that we can get that fabulous job. It is extremely hard to see yourself reaching for the stars if you don't believe you are worth the effort. Self-esteem, both positive and negative, has a huge impact on how we dream.

> The only thing that will stop you
> fulfilling your dream is you.
> *Tom Bradley*

Remember the ancient Hebrew saying that goes like this: 'As a man thinks in his heart, so he is.' If we think that we don't deserve to have good things happen to us, then we won't let them happen. We won't dream of amazing things happening to us because we just don't believe we are worth it. On the other hand, if we believe that we do deserve to have good things happen to us, then they will. Sportsmen and women who believe in themselves can see themselves winning that fight, receiving the champion's cup, being awarded the gold medal. This process is called visualisation and sportsmen and women have used it for years.

> You've got to chase your dreams.
> *Earvin 'Magic' Johnson*

This process of visualisation is how our dreams take shape. As we believe in our heart, so we are, and eventually will become. If we continually cry poor, guess who's going to stay poor? If we believe that we always get cheated, then guess who will be the first one to be cheated next time. Or if we continually believe that we are worthless, useless, good for nothing, then that is how we will treat ourselves. When people see us treat ourselves in a certain way, we are unconsciously giving them permission to do the same.

> Go confidently in the direction of your dreams.
> Live the life you've always imagined.
> *Henry David Thoreau*

If you continually absorb negative thoughts, your world will become nothing but a rubbish dump. Garbage in means garbage out! Thinking of good things, things that are noble, things that are uplifting, things that bring joy, comfort and peace of mind – surprise, surprise – these are the things that will make you fly.

A tragic example of the consequences of garbage in, garbage out is the Columbine High School massacre that occurred in the United States on 20 April 1999. Two students entered their school and shot twelve students and a teacher dead, injured 24 others and then turned the guns on themselves. In the police investigation that followed, it was revealed that the two students, Eric Harris and Dylan Klebold, were fixated on violence. They lived on a staple diet of bloody, gory murder movies. An American study which examined the effect of young children viewing violence on TV showed that it increased the chances of them re-enacting that same level of violence in later life. As Eric Harris and Dylan Klebold so sadly and graphically illustrated, what you think about you live out!

Making the dream real

If we can conceive of something in our mind, and then begin to believe it in our heart, we will achieve it in our life: conceive – believe – achieve.

Another way of making a dream become real is to visualise it and then write it down. There is an ancient Hebrew adage that says: 'Write the vision down and make it plain that he may run who reads it.'

I like the part about the person who reads it, will run. What do they mean by that? It means that those who read the vision that has been written down will get it and run with it. That is what happens when you write your own vision down, you become accountable for it to happen. You have made a commitment to yourself by recording it, and you can then go back to it and keep refreshing your enthusiasm when times do get a little tough.

> If you can dream it you can do it.
> Always remember, this whole thing
> started with a mouse.
> *Walt Disney*

A price tag

Dreams often have a price tag attached. If fulfilling a dream were easy, everybody would be doing it. Making a dream a reality takes something – everything you've got!

It requires sacrifice, commitment, focus and having a positive, supportive group of people around you. On the flipside, that's all it takes!

A dream's individual price tag depends on the dream. Some dreams are extremely costly emotionally, but reasonably inexpensive financially; others may be expensive financially, but less so emotionally. Some are extremely costly in time, like my dream of becoming the NSW State boxing champion. Although it only cost me $32 to register, about $12 a week in gym fees and petrol money, it took a huge time commitment from me to train every single day, twice a day, for seven years. It also took the support of my wife and kids, along with the support of my coach and training partners. The biggest expense for me was time, followed by the emotional cost of maintaining the disciplined training and fighting that was needed if I were to win. In the end I did, and it was well worth the cost!

> Most people never run far enough on their first wind to find out they've got a second.
> Give your dreams all you've got and you'll be amazed at the energy that comes out of you.
> *William James*

So, having said all this, we need to be wise. What value do you place on your dream? All dreams are achievable, but you have to count the cost to see if you can afford it. You have to look at the end product rationally, decide if your dream is worth the cost and then, if it is, make the commitment. At the end of the day, any dream worth achieving is worth the sacrifice!

> Some men see things as they are
> And ask why. Others dream of things
> That never were and ask why not!
> *George Bernard Shaw*

Dreams were meant to come true

One morning Henry Ford, founder of the Ford automotive group back around the turn of the last century, called a meeting with his production staff and chief engineers. He had dreamed of an engine, he told them, the likes of which no-one had ever seen, an engine so wild in its conception that all of the production staff and engineers laughed it off as simply impossible. Henry Ford, driven by his passion for motor vehicles, had a dream to see a V8 engine in one of the cars that bore his name. Henry would meet his staff regularly and ask, 'Gentlemen, where is my engine?'

The staff would reply, 'It's impossible.'

Ford's response was stern but sure: 'If you think you can, or you think you can't, either way you are right!' Then he'd walk out of the room.

Fourteen years later the first mass-produced V8 engine in the world was developed and produced by Ford.

I truly believe that dreams were meant to come true. Jules Verne dreamed of a submarine well before anyone attempted to build one. Leonardo da Vinci designed flying machines centuries before the Wright brothers pulled it off. Dr Martin Luther King had a dream of equal civil rights for all African Americans. President John F Kennedy believed that a man could be put on the moon. How many people dreamed of that?

> A man is not old until regrets
> take the place of dreams.
> *John Barrymore*

There are many things that have happened throughout history because someone had a dream. Why would we be capable of having dreams if we weren't capable of fulfilling them? We are creative beings. I look around the Sydney skyscape and marvel. I look at the rail system, the water delivery system, all developed in the past two hundred years or so to create the most beautiful city in the world. Take a look at the telecommunications systems – far out! Thirty years ago a cartoonist dreamed that his character, Dick Tracey, had a watch that was also a phone. Today there are watches that are also phones and soon could be even more. We dream because we have the potential to take that dream and make it a reality.

What I've learnt

- Your dream is what will carry you on your life's journey.
- Our dreams are birthed from deep-seated passions and desires.
- The way you think and the way you see yourself affect your dreams. You have to think positive and believe in yourself for your dreams to come true.
- Dreams have a price, but any dream worth achieving is worth the cost.
- Value your dream and go after it. It is within you and it is has the potential to come true.

Dreams do come true: Jennifer Capriati

Jennifer Capriati was born in New York in the USA in 1976 to Italian immigrant parents. She made her professional tennis debut in 1990 at the tender age of thirteen. She did really well in competitions almost immediately and soon shot up the WTA rankings to become the youngest seed in Wimbledon history and the youngest top ten ranked player four months before her fifteenth birthday. By 1992 she had won an Olympic Gold medal, passed the $1 million mark in earnings after becoming Wimbledon's youngest ever semi-finalist, and won the Canadian Open. (She had actually won US$2.5 million by this stage.)

However the pressure of being this teen sensation, this phenomenal young player, seemed to get the better of her. In 1993 Jennifer announced she was taking a break from tennis as it wasn't fun any more. Later that year Jennifer was arrested for stealing a $22 ring from a Miami shopping mall – not a $22 000 ring or even a $2200 ring, a $22 ring!

Things went from bad to worse for Jennifer when in 1994 she was arrested again, this time for the possession of marijuana. Her police mug shot became the face of teenage tennis burnouts around the world, and would follow her wherever she went.

In 1996 Jennifer Capriati decided to make her return to the WTA tour. It would be a slow and arduous task, but by 2001 the fairytale comeback was complete. Jennifer Capriati realised her potential by winning the Australian Tennis Open and beating world number one Martina Hingis to do it. She was only 24. Jennifer then went on to win the French Open later that year. She came back to Melbourne in 2002 and defended her

Australian Open crown, again beating Martina Hingis in the final.

After winning the Australian Open in 2001, Jennifer Capriati was quoted by *The Sun-Herald* as saying, 'Who would have thought I would ever have made it here after so much has happened? If you believe in yourself anything can happen. It shows that dreams do come true.'

7
Connections

Inherent in every intention and desire, is the mechanics for its fulfilment ... Intention and desire have infinite power. And when we introduce an intention to the fertile ground of pure potentiality, we put the infinite power to work in us.

Deepak Chopra

Are the parts connected?

This chapter is going to be brief with a simple, straightforward message: your dream needs to be attached to your life. If the canopy of your hot-air balloon isn't attached to your gondola, nothing will get off the ground! If you just have a beautiful canopy (a dream) and a solid gondola (your base) without a connection between them you might as well have an oversized picnic blanket and picnic basket – and neither can fly!

If you want your dream to take off, you need to make it possible for it to happen. If your dream is about becoming an astronaut, yet you are living a life that has nothing to do with aeronautics – the study of outer space, astro-physics and so on – then your dream will never take off. You have to make sure that the way you live is connected to what you want to do. For example, I want to be the best youth communicator in history because I'm passionate about youth issues. So what do I do on a daily basis? I speak to and hang out with young people; I pay attention to their world and their needs. To achieve success you need to connect your life and your dream.

> Do what you feel in your heart to be right –
> for you'll be criticised anyway. You'll be
> damned if you do and damned if you don't.
> *Eleanor Roosevelt*

Why do I have to connect the parts?

It is important to understand why your base and your dream have to be connected. If you take your life in a different direction to your dream, your energy will be divided – your desire will say to go one way, your actions will lead you in another and the end result will be stress, resentment, bitterness and anger. These can manifest in apathy, laziness and negative, critical attitudes which will turn you into one big sourpuss! That's why as you live your day-to-day life, your thoughts, your intentions, your actions must all direct your attention and energy towards your dream.

The strength of the connection between balloon and basket is also extremely important. Imagine you are flying in a hot-air balloon, high in the sky, when suddenly you realise that the basket is attached to the balloon by threads of cotton, not thick cables! Not a very reassuring thought is it? Similarly you must ensure the connection between your life and your dream is sturdy and strong or it could all come crashing down. It's all well and good to have a desire, a passion, but without putting that passion in to *real* action by connecting the way we live to the fulfilment of the dream, then that's what it will remain – just a desire.

Keep it real

Although I am encouraging you to dream and dream big, make sure the way you approach achieving your dream is realistic. If you have been someone who would never have dared to dream of doing something significant in history but now you are beginning to explore the possibilities, take it a step at a time. I suggest that you don't try to build a balloon capable of crossing the Atlantic on your first attempt! Build a balloon that you can pilot easily. As each dream becomes a reality, then build bigger next time.

> Persistence is to the character
> of man as carbon is to steel.
> *Napoleon Hill*

If you attempt something too outrageous first time around, chances are you might be overwhelmed by the size of the task. If you attempt anything way beyond your ability too early, you could fall short and, if you are not prepared, this could end in discouragement and hurt. If this happened, you might not want to attempt anything else. You could damage your confidence needlessly and therefore sabotage any remaining hope of fulfilling your goals – all because you went too hard too fast.

> You make up your mind before you start
> that sacrifice is part of the package.
> *Richard M DeVos*

Putting it into practice

I have found that when I want to accomplish something new and challenging, my life has to change. That's not really a profound revelation, I know. But you would be surprised by the number of people who don't see the need to change their day-to-day life if their goal is to be reached. If you want to do something new, you've got to do something new! To get fit, you have to train. Now that might mean a change in sleep patterns because you may have to get up earlier to go to the gym. You most certainly will be more tired at the end of the day so you'll go to bed earlier. Sometimes the obvious things you need to do are the hardest to see.

> When you do the common things in
> life in an uncommon way, then you will
> command the attention of the world.
> *George Washington Carver*

You also have to plan. My dad once told me of a quote from Benjamin Franklin: 'By failing to prepare, you are preparing to fail.' This makes a lot of sense. If you don't go onto the field with a game plan, you'll be forced to play to the plan of the opposition. That means that they will dictate the terms, and you will always be on the back foot, playing catch-up.

When formulating your plan, the best way to go about it is to firstly articulate what it is that you want to achieve and write it down. The next step is to note where you are in relation to this dream becoming a reality. Then write down the steps you think you will need to take to reach your goal. Note all the sacrifices and costs that will need to be made, including money, time, energy, training and other education. Write them down in chronological order from where you are now to where you want to be.

The big dream might actually be a couple of years away, so what you can do is highlight certain milestones along the way and see these as smaller goals which are easier to achieve. As you reach each of these goals, you will become more confident that you can attain the bigger prize, the ultimate goal. The best thing about this process is that when you finally get to your ultimate goal, winning and success and hard work will have become such a way of life for you and your confidence will have grown to such a degree that bigger, more radical dreams will become more achievable.

What I've learnt

- Dreams and life have to be connected. If they are not, then life won't fulfil the dream.
- Make sure the connection between life and dream is not just a flimsy thought process but that it is thought and action put together.
- Match your dream to your ability and desire. Don't try and live someone else's dream. Sure, stretch yourself, but don't break yourself.
- To do something new, you have to do something new. Positive change brings about positive change.
- Don't plan to fail by failing to plan. Have a goal, make a plan, and go for it.

Living the dream: Richard Branson

Most media reports will tell you that Sir Richard Branson is a flamboyant British entrepreneur, a billionaire, a man with an insatiable appetite for starting new business and so on.

I think Sir Richard Branson is much more than this. He seems almost consumed with a passion for making things happen, and making things fun. Every company that has his Virgin brand on it seems to reflect his enthusiastic passion for life. This is a guy born into a family who, as he puts it, would die for each other but had very little money. This is a guy who by the age of sixteen was publishing a student magazine and then started a mail order record company that became the genesis of the now famous Virgin empire. Twenty years later, in 1992, Thorn EMI bought Virgin Records for US$1 billion!

Sir Richard's successes are numerous, from record-breaking attempts in hot-air balloons to the development of telecommunication companies and airlines. The guy lives what he believes, and he is a down-to-earth bloke as well – not at all conceited but very, very approachable and likeable. I had the privilege of meeting him once when he launched his Virgin Money arm of the Virgin Group in Australia. He then went on to appear on a variety show 'Rove Live' which was being broadcast from someone's house just down the road from where I lived.

When I met Sir Richard, I couldn't help but realise that this guy's life is totally connected to his dream. He was once quoted as saying, 'Sometimes I do wake up in the mornings and feel like I've just had the most incredible dream. I've just dreamt my life.'

Sir Richard is always looking for ways in which he can have a positive impact on the world. He dares to venture into areas where the market is dominated by a few big players who are exploiting the consumer. Sir Richard Branson is the ultimate example of what planning, dreaming and living life connected to the dream can achieve.

8
The fuel tanks

What lies behind us and what
lies before us are small matters
compared to what lies within us.
Ralph Waldo Emerson

Ignite the passion

The next thing we need to get our balloon to fly is fuel. We have a solid gondola with a strong connection to the canopy. Now what else do we need to get it to fly? Fuel, of course! It would be no use assembling a balloon, if you hadn't planned to get it into the air! To do that you need fuel. So where can we find fuel? Fuel is the motivation behind our dream, it is our passion. Passion is the fuel that drives the dream. It is the vital component that has been there since the beginning, but now it is time to put it in place and ignite it!

To live a passionate life, you really need to have an understanding of what passion actually is. The passion I am talking about is defined by the Macquarie Dictionary as 'a strong or extravagant fondness, enthusiasm, or desire for anything'. Webster's Dictionary also defines it as 'an irrational but irresistible motive for a belief or action'.

I like to think of passion as the stuff inside you that you can't really put into words but you know is there. It is something that you can feel but can never quite articulate. It's what drives you to achieve your goals and fulfil your dreams. So this is where and how passion fits into the balloon analogy.

A hot-air balloon with no fuel looks good, might even be of sound construction, but she ain't goin' nowhere. It is the fuel, when ignited, which lifts the hot-air balloon and then determines the altitude to which the balloon will rise. The fuel for our dream is, as I said, our passion. Our passion gives us the energy we need for lift-off, the energy we need to pursue our dream. Put another way, our dreams are born from what we are passionate about.

> Without a sense of urgency, desire loses its value.
> *Jim Rohn*

Putting passion into action

Take a look at one of the definitions of passion again: 'An irrational but irresistible motive for a belief or action.' Irrational but irresistible, that's what passion is – irresistible. Many people, even those close to me, have suggested that the course of action I was about to take to fulfil my dream of running DARE:Ops was irrational. 'Do you really know what you are doing?' they would ask.

Does starting a business aimed at helping young people find their passion and dreams, then daring to empower as many of them as possible in order to launch a new generation of ground breakers, history makers and planet shakers sound rational? No, and at times it didn't even seem rational to me.

Still, setting off with nothing but a heart full of passion and a head full of dreams is exactly what I did. Was it easy? No way! Has it been worth it? You bet. In the past four years I have learnt more about myself, more about my wife and my family and friends, those who support and believe in me, and more about those who think I'm stark raving mad, than I have in the past ten years. I have been through trials and tribulations. I know what it is like to look in the cupboard and see nothing but a packet of sugar to feed my wife and kids. I know how it feels to receive an eviction notice. There was a time when we received seven eviction notices in eighteen months. Talk about stress!

> The future belongs to those who
> believe in the beauty of their dreams.
> *Eleanor Roosevelt*

I put myself and my family on the line because of my passion. You see, although it seemed irrational, there was something so flipping *irresistible* about this dream that I simply had to pursue it.

> We shall draw from the heart of suffering itself
> the means of inspiration and survival.
> *Sir Winston Churchill*

The DARE story

The DARE charity story is one of humble beginnings and started when I was only a youth myself. After leaving school in Year 10 I found myself being asked to speak at surfing competitions to rally guys to volunteer as judges for the next heat. That then became requests for me to be a beach announcer or MC at competitions. These invites soon became requests to speak at youth groups, schools and other community functions, motivating young people. I was even asked by a political party to speak at their rallies doing youth-to-youth presentations! That's where my political interests started.

I began running surf camps a few years later, all the while earning myself a trade in vehicle painting. The camps were ad-hoc at best, but heaps of fun. The camps became known as campDARE, which eventually morphed into the name we are known by now, DARE:Ops. Then I decided to run as a candidate in the 2003 NSW election. This earned me quite a bit of publicity, as I was young and appealed directly to the youth market. However, I lost that election and needed to find a new direction. As I still had the desire to motivate young people I decided that I was going to turn my passion into a full-time career, motivating youth through camps and seminars.

After all, how could I motivate others if I was on the dole living off government handouts?

However, I soon realised that I couldn't be a very effective motivational speaker and youth motivator with a family that was starving and had no roof over their heads, so I bit the bullet. I went down to the local Centrelink to apply for the dole. However, the spirit of helplessness there was so overwhelming I couldn't go through with it. But I knew I had to *earn* some sort of income. After all, how could I motivate others if I was on the dole living off government handouts? I could just see myself talking to a group of kids and saying, 'Yeah, live your dream. Look at me, I'm a dole bludger! I can't even do it! But follow me!'

I wanted to go it alone and make a name for myself among schools throughout our nation. I believed in myself and the message I had to share. I thought after my election exposure schools would be lining up to book me. Everything I wanted to share is my own experience and my own material – surely teachers would see the value in that! Not so! You have to have credibility and recognition. I didn't realise that even though I was recognisable, I wasn't recognised! The teachers didn't know if I could communicate effectively with their students just because they had seen me as a political candidate on TV! This was a major stumbling block. So how do you get the recognition you need to make a living as a youth motivator? You do freebies – speaking engagements for no pay but which build your reputation so that when you get asked back you can then request a fee.

> View stumbling blocks as
> stepping stones to the stars.
> *Unknown*

However this doesn't pay the rent. So I was forced to take a builder's labouring job to cover expenses. It didn't pay much and I hated it, but it put food on the table, plus the physical labour kept me fit. So, while hoisting bags of cement over my shoulder for hours at a time, I was dreaming, fuelling my passion to live my dream, and thinking of ways to make it a reality.

> Impossible is a word found only in the dictionary
> of fools.
> *Unknown*

Sometimes to get to where you want to go you have to do what you hate doing. In the beginning I saw spending a day on a building site as simply a waste of time, losing nine hours a day where I could have been communicating with sponsors, ringing schools and talking to principals and careers advisors, connecting with and inspiring young people. I didn't want to be busting my guts shovelling dirt and cement, moving tonnes of metal and operating sanding machines and jackhammers. However, it did give me plenty of time to think and dream. This is where you have to look for the good in every situation. Stay positive, that's the key.

So I pressed on, all the while continuing to look for opportunities that would help me get out of the situation I was in and get on with my dream of helping young people find their destiny.

Guess what!

The passion I had for youth, coupled with the passionate hate for the labouring I was doing, gave me the drive to organise a camp that was supported by sponsors. It was also filmed by a national television network and shown on their news and current affairs program with an exceptional response from the public. Now, I was able to secure this exposure because of a person I had met during the 2003 election. During a random phone call, the opportunity arose for me to share my thoughts and ideas about a camp I was running, and the next thing you know, I get national TV exposure, not only for the kids and the camp, but for myself as a youth motivator. I have since made the most of other opportunities that have come my way. These have allowed me to write, direct and produce my own surf movie called *Firestorm*. I then went on to take the ten young men across the Kokoda Track in Papua New Guinea which I have previously mentioned. We became the second fastest non-military team to cross the track, doing the trip in a gruelling six days. This too was filmed and shown on national television, and you know the story from there.

> What we vividly imagine, ardently desire, enthusiastically act upon, must inevitably come to pass.
> *Colin P Sisson*

I have since run five camps in outer city suburbs that have been the location for some pretty serious civil unrest in recent times. In cooperation with the local police and schools, these camps have had an amazing impact on the young people we work with. Some of the activities have again attracted media attention with three cover stories in six months on national television. If you allow your passion to drive you in a positive direction, positive things happen. Only very recently I secured a sponsorship from Reebok and Macquarie Group agreed to financially support the camps that I run through DARE:Ops. Right now you are reading this book! Hopefully you are being inspired to have a go, to act on your passion. If you are already doing that, I

If you allow your passion to drive you in a positive direction, positive things happen.

want to dare you to step it up a cog, go harder, do more, and do it better. You have what it takes – allow *your* passion to drive you!

So what is your passion?

Here is a simple test that may help you identify what it is that you are passionate about. Ask yourself: What is the thing that grabs my interest totally, the minute I hear or see something relating to it? What is it that sets me on fire inside that makes me feel alive? What is the thing I can't wait to do again?

Now, don't pay attention to those negative voices in your head which say, 'That's a stupid idea. You could never do that.' Ignore them! Remember the truth. You can do it. Somebody has to do it, so it might as well be you!

> If you are not willing to risk the unusual, you will have to settle for the ordinary.
> *Jim Rohn*

Maybe take a few moments right now to take a good hard look at yourself and your desires. Grab a book, a piece of paper or a business card. Write down what your passion is. When you do that, you will have taken the first steps towards turning your passion into a tangible reality. If you choose not to do anything about your passion, it will die. Not only that, it could come back and try to stop those around you with similar passions fulfilling their dreams. People who don't take any action about their dreams and passions bury them so deep, they forget they even had one in the first place.

It takes courage

There is a line at the beginning of the movie *Braveheart* that I love. Young William Wallace sees his father and brother brought home on a horse-drawn wagon, both slain in a battle, fighting for what they believed in. Young William has a dream. In the dream he is lying on a table in a hut that looks like the equivalent of a medieval morgue. His dead father is lying on the table next to him. Then, William's father seemingly comes to life, turns his head and looks at William and says to the young boy, 'Your heart is free. Have the courage to follow it!'

Do you want to follow your heart? Do you want to allow your passion to drive you? Then you will have to be courageous. Let me ask you a question. Why do the people around us tend to complain when we move forward in life? There is no difference between your life and theirs. We all have the same opportunities. We all breathe the same air. As the saying goes, 'The billionaire and the beggar have the same amount of hours in the day.'

Why do the people around us tend to complain when we move forward in life?

I believe the reason others start complaining when you progress is that you expose them. You make them uncomfortable because they have the same obstacles and opportunities as you do, or they did, and they haven't done anything about it. They have chosen to stay content with the average, 'status quo' life that they are used to living, the life they are *comfortable* with. They too have the potential to be great, but have chosen not to be. And now that their excuses for not doing anything are exposed for what they are, they have a choice: stay where they are or follow your lead and move forward. Instead of daring to believe they too can follow their passion and do great things, most people choose to stay in their rut. And because some people are uncomfortable seeing someone they thought was less than they are now leading the way, they may try to drag you down, chop you down to size and put you in your place. You will have to find the courage to resist this.

Unfortunately as you grow, some will grow with you and others will remain the same. It's not up to you to change others or drag them along with you. In this life you are the pilot. You never see an eagle carrying a galah around on its back, now do you? Neither bird would get off the ground. Find the courage to go fly and others will naturally follow. Become an eagle and you will find yourself soaring with other eagles.

> **You never see an eagle carrying a galah around on its back, now do you?**

> Take the first step in faith. You don't have to see the whole staircase, just take the first step in faith.
> *Martin Luther King Jnr*

So, have you written down what your passion is? Then you have dared to take the first step towards turning your passion into reality. Now you are ready to fire up your balloon and take flight.

> Whatever the mind can conceive
> and believe, the mind can achieve.
> *Napoleon Hill*

What I've learnt

- We need to identify our passion if we want our dream to become a reality.
- Ignite your passion. It is the fuel, the energy source, which will drive your dream.
- Good things can come from bad situations.
- People will bag you out and doubt you. Don't doubt yourself. Have the courage to follow your heart.

Crikey, what passion: Steve Irwin

I don't think there is a better example of an individual whose passion drove his dream to become a reality than the late, great Steve Irwin. He was the quintessential man of passion.

Steve Irwin was passionate about wildlife, wilderness and conservation. If you could bottle his enthusiasm and sell it, you'd be a billionaire. He had so much fuel in his tanks that at 44, the age when he died, many kids would have found it difficult keeping up with him.

He was a blond-haired eight-year-old when he left Victoria and relocated with his family to Beerwah in Queensland. Here his father opened up a family business, the family reptile park later named Australia Zoo. By the time Steve was nine, Irwin senior had taught him how to trap wild crocodiles at night in the rivers of northern Queensland. One of Steve's proudest boasts was that every croc in the zoo had either been caught by him or hand-raised in the zoo. That's over 100 crocodiles!

With his famous trademark saying of 'Crikey', Steve the 'Croc Hunter' Irwin became a smash hit in America where his first documentary and then his television series was aired on the Discovery Channel. The show made the Irwin family television personalities in several continents.

Steve was so passionate about reptiles that he wrote sixteen scientific papers on them. His television shows have been seen by more than 200 million viewers in 120 countries around the globe, and he even appeared in the movie *Dr Dolittle 2* with Eddie Murphy. Not only was Steve passionate about animal conservation and reptiles, he was passionately in love with his wife Terri, and let everybody know it, and he adored his two children, Bindi and Bob.

Tragically Steve died on 4 September 2006 while filming a documentary called *Ocean's Deadliest*. It was estimated that over 300 million viewers across the globe tuned in to watch Steve's memorial service held at his beloved Australia Zoo.

Passion is the fuel that fires up dreams. Steve Irwin had plenty of it!

BUT I WANT CONTROL OVER EVERY HUMAN THAT INFESTS THIS HORRIBLE, PATHETIC LITTLE PLANET!!!
THIS IS A RECURRING THEME WITH YOU SATAN. I WONDER IF YOU SHOULD TRY SOMETHING A LITTLE LESS AMBITIOUS... LIKE CONTROL OF ALL LAWYERS...?

9
The pilot

I could not, at any age, be content to take my place by the fireside and simply look on. Life was meant to be lived. Curiosity must be kept alive. One must never, for whatever reason, turn his back on life.

Eleanor Roosevelt

Who's driving this thing?

Next in our balloon analogy we have the pilot – that's you. There are many people out there that wouldn't be able to dream up an original thought or idea, even if they had a late night with a few beers and a bad pizza! But they will take your idea in the blink of an eye and call it their own. You have got to be the pilot of your dream, especially when people come alongside making all kinds of promises and offering all kinds of input.

When I first started to approach people and organisations for backing to make my surf movie, one guy in particular was very enthusiastic about helping me. He approached the organisation he worked for to get funding and arranged for me to meet the managing director.

Then he started to get a little too enthusiastic, coming up with ideas such as making a trilogy of movies covering surfing, skating and snow boarding. He was taking the movie off its original course. Because he felt he'd done so much to help my dream take flight, even though he actually hadn't done much at all, he felt he had the right to fly the dream. That is simply not how it should be. The passion, the fuel, is yours, and the dream belongs to you.

> **You know just what is needed to get your balloon in the air. That's why *you* have to be the pilot of the dream.**

You know just what is needed to get your balloon in the air. That's why *you* have to be the pilot of the dream. It is the pilot in a hot-air balloon who is in charge of the fuel.

Beware the dream hijackers – they can be anywhere!

When you start putting together the pieces that will make your dream a reality, the world will start to notice. And there will be those who like what they see just a little too much. This is where you will have to protect not only yourself but your dream from those who will try to take it from you. To protect your dream, sometimes you have to be selfish about it. You worked hard for it, you put the effort in, you made the sacrifice, you made the necessary changes, so no-one has the right to tell you what you can and cannot do with your dream.

Like a parent with their child, you have got to be protective, even overprotective at times! It takes hard work and dedication to make a dream become a reality. Don't let some 'Johnny-come-lately' jump into your gondola and tell you where to go or, even worse, take over the controls. They don't have the passion – you do. Remember the passion is the fuel you need to keep your dream aloft. Without the right amount of fuel, the dream will crash and burn, and the pilot and passengers will go down with the lot.

With the same passion you are fuelling your dream, you must protect your dream. After all, it is all yours.

> It is not fair to ask of others what you are not willing to do yourself.
> *Eleanor Roosevelt*

This is all yours – so protect it with all your might

At the end of the day, this is all yours. Your effort, your dream, your desire, your ability, your ideas, your passion, your enterprise, your convictions, your discipline, your sacrifice, your determination, your drive, your life. Are you going to let someone come in and simply take it? I think not! With the same passion you are fuelling your dream, you must protect your dream. After all, it is all yours.

> In the middle of difficulty lies opportunity.
> *Albert Einstein*

Your chance to lead

In the midst of the struggle to work with people who want to support you, as well as watching out for those that are just along for a free ride, there lies an incredible opportunity for you to learn to be a leader, to be the captain of the ship. You can't shut everyone out, but you obviously can't have everyone aboard as well. The decision is yours. Leadership decisions like this can be frightening, but don't let them scare you. I have seen people faced with this type of decision who let the situation overwhelm them. What happened to their dream? *Nothing!* Their dream never took off because they didn't step up to the plate to pilot it. It's better to have a go and fail trying than to never have a go at all.

> **Leadership decisions like this can be frightening, but don't let them scare you.**

> Twenty years from now you will be more disappointed by the things you didn't do than by the ones you did ...
> *Mark Twain*

What I've learnt

- You have to pilot your own dream. You set the course.
- Be protective of your dream, especially against people who see the effort you put in and try to hijack your work.

- There is a place for selfishness; use it to guard your dream.
- Find the balance – work with a team but protect your dream. This is your opportunity to lead, Captain!

Steering the dream: Casey Stoner

Casey Stoner is a young man who knows how to steer himself in the direction he wants to go. Growing up in a motorbike-mad family, he learnt to ride at the age of three and competed in his first dirt bike event in the under nines category at the age of four. By the time he was six he had won his first Australian title.

From that time on until he turned fourteen Casey travelled the country with his incredibly supportive family and won an amazing 41 Australian dirt and long track titles and over 70 state titles, riding up to five different bikes in a meeting in different categories. Once, at the age of twelve, Casey raced in the Australian long track titles in five different categories with seven rounds in each engine capacity that made up the category, a total of 35 races in one weekend. He won 32 of the 35 races and took out five national titles in the one meet!

After his fourteenth birthday Casey and his family moved to the UK because here he was the legal age to road race whereas he couldn't road race in Australia until he turned sixteen. He took to road racing like a duck to water and the sponsors took to him. In 2000, his first year of road racing, he won the English 125cc Aprilia championship. He also rode two roads of the Spanish championship that year as well.

Casey Stoner was a very young man who knew which direction in life he wanted to travel and how to get there. He put in the hard yards and he was the pilot of his dream. He went on to race for the Telefonica Movistar team in the Spanish championships the following year. He raced in both English and Spanish championships that year and finished second in both, also securing two wild card entries in the MotoGP

125cc World Series in England and Australia. The next year, 2002, Casey was invited to race in the 250cc World Series at the tender age of sixteen. In 2003 he rode in the 125cc MotoGP series for Lucio Cecchinello and Sefilo Oxydo LCR and won his first Grand Prix (GP) at Valencia.

From there Casey went on in 2004 to ride for KTM in the now familiar 125cc MotoGP World Series and gave KTM their first ever GP win and made it to the podium six times that year. In 2005 Casey came back to Aprilia team, this time in the 250cc GP World Series where he won in Portugal, Shanghai, Qatar, Sepang and Istanbul.

Finally in 2006 at the mere age of 20 Casey Stoner accomplished his ambition to ride in the quickest and most prestigious class of motorcycle racing MotoGP. Now he was with the big boys, Valentino Rossi, Marco Melandri, Kenny Roberts Jnr and the rest of the best riders in the world. He set pole position in only his second MotoGP race in Qatar, and Casey finished eighth in his rookie year in MotoGP.

Casey is now riding for Ducati, and is now Australia's newest motorcycle world champion following on from Mick Doohan and Wayne Gardner before him. Just reading about Casey's achievements can leave you short of breath. He is certainly a young man who knows how to pilot his own dream.

10
The ground crew

Truly great friends are hard to find,
difficult to leave, and impossible
to forget.
G Randolf

So why do I need a ground crew?

When you fly a hot-air balloon, you need ground crew. A ground crew is made up of a group of people who help the pilot prepare to take the balloon to the skies. The ground crew are responsible for assembling the balloon on the ground, and then holding it securely until it is ready to lift-off.

Now remember, each section of the balloon in the analogy represents a section of our preparation to achieve our dreams. So what do you think the ground crew represents? Who keeps you balanced and safe until you are ready to fly by yourself? Who makes sure you can land safely when you return?

You have probably guessed it by now. The ground crew in our life are people, usually our friends. As the crew are situated around the gondola on a hot-air balloon, keeping it safe, on course and realising the balloon's potential, so the people we choose to have in our life can do the same for you and your dream.

We have already discussed the value of having great friends and partnerships in Chapter 4. Not only do they enrich your life, they can be of great help in achieving your dream. Now let's look more closely at the role our friends, or our ground crew, can play in helping us to go after our dreams.

> I light my candle from
> their torches.
> *Robert Burton*

Is a ground crew really necessary?

Now, one of the roles of the ground crew in flying hot-air balloons is to hold the balloon down. But why would you want to have something tied around your home base, your gondola, that is going to just hold you back? What's the use in that? The answer is simple. The ground crew only hold you down until you, the pilot, tell them you are ready to fly.

Your ground crew help you make sure you start *on* course and are travelling in the right direction. A ground crew will also help you stay on the ground if the weather conditions are too dangerous to fly. Ground crews keep you safe. That's their role! So are they necessary? Absolutely!

Recently, my local daily paper ran a story on a hot-air balloon tragedy in Vancouver, Canada. Two of the eleven passengers died after the balloon burst into flames as it was preparing to launch.

The ground crew were holding onto the tethers when suddenly the propane gas tanks ignited, turning the gondola into a fireball and threatened to shoot skywards. Although the tethers that the ground crew were holding were burning swiftly, they managed to hold onto them long enough so the majority of the passengers could escape before the balloon was engulfed in flames and plummeted back to earth. If the ground crew hadn't held on as long as they had the death toll may well have been higher.

> Friendship doubles your joy
> and divides your grief.
> *Swedish proverb*

Who should be in my crew?

To know if someone is really a part of your ground crew is simple. How do they react to your dreams? Are they supportive or destructive? Do they stand by you when you attempt to take off, or are they hoping to see you crash and burn?

> A true friend knows your weaknesses but shows
> you your strengths; feels your fears but fortifies
> your faith; sees your anxieties but frees your spirit;
> recognises your disabilities but emphasises your
> possibilities.
> *William Arthur Ward*

Can family be part of my crew?

Just because someone is related to you doesn't necessarily
mean that they are automatically a part of your ground
crew. Here's a true story that demonstrates why having a
family member as part of your crew doesn't always work.

Warren (not his real name) inherited the family
business with his older brother. Now the business
had just lost over a million dollars in a bad business
deal. However, Warren has an incredible gift of seeing
business opportunities and making them profitable
very quickly. He single-handedly took the business and
saw it expand from a modest carpentry and building
company to a multi-million dollar organisation with at
least five different divisions.

You would think that Warren's older brother would
be proud of his younger sibling. After watching all of
Warren's marketing ideas turn into massive profits and
observing his younger brother invest countless hours
into the business, you think he would be thrilled
to see the business turn around from the edge of
collapse, to grow into a very powerful development
group. *You'd think!* Unfortunately, the person who

attacked Warren the most, humiliated him in front of staff and undermined his authority, was his older brother.

Warren then made an incredibly courageous decision – he left the family business that he loved so dearly and took up an offer from a business associate, who believed in Warren and his abilities. Warren had to make the decision to replace a member of his ground crew who wasn't helping him in his dreams, with someone who had faith in him and offered his support.

The pay-off for Warren has been fantastic. In the first five months of working in his new job, his efforts alone saw the company double the work output they had produced the previous year. In turn his boss keeps Warren on course, lends advice when needed, reins him in if particular situations seem dangerous, and generally allows Warren to fly to his potential. At the end of the day, everybody wins.

> An idealist is a person
> who helps other people
> to be prosperous.
> *Henry Ford*

What they do and what they don't do

As you can see, your ground crew can help you reach your destination. The people in your life that fulfil this role will be supportive, loving, and generous with their time for you. They will always have an ear to hear you out and encourage you. A ground crew member will never manipulate you to do something for *their* personal gain either. They are by your side because they love and care for you and want to support you. If you make a mistake, they will help you rise from it, without ridiculing or bagging you out. If they hear people saying negative things behind your back, they will defend you.

However, it's good to remember that a supportive person in your life will be encouraging, but only toward that which is going to be of real lasting benefit to you. If something will bring short-term reward but long-term pain and despair, a ground crew member will never say 'Go for it!'. On the other hand, if a bit of sacrifice, hard work and discipline is needed, to see you reach your goal and live your dream, then your ground crew will most certainly encourage you to 'Get off your butt!'.

> In order to make friends
> you must first be friendly!
> *Dale Carnegie*

The members of your ground crew are your defenders, as you should be for them. This is not a one-way street. If you want someone to be a ground crew member for you, you also need to be one for them!

Choose your crew wisely

We have already discussed how you will need to choose your ground crew wisely, as they can have a huge impact on the decisions you make about your dreams. And as you can see, they also have a huge influence on whether you can achieve your dreams safely and with support. But in the end, this is your life, your journey. How high you want to fly (if you want to fly at all) and who you want along for the ride is ultimately your choice.

What I've learnt

- A ground crew is necessary as without them you could spin out of control.
- Just because someone is related doesn't automatically make them a member of your ground crew.
- A ground crew is made of people in your life who keep you on track to fulfil your dream; they will also protect you when it's too dangerous to fly.
- A ground crew member is looking after your interests first and foremost, no hidden agendas.
- At the end of the day, who you choose to be a member of your ground crew is totally up to you.

Drop the dead weights: Shannan Taylor

Shannan Taylor knows what it is like to have people 'hang' around for all the wrong reasons. A former world number one boxer in the junior middleweight division, in 2001 he fought the best pound-for-pound fighter in the world at the time, 'Sugar' Shane Mosley.

Shannan was paid $1 million for that fight, which unfortunately he lost. What he gained was a raft of new 'friends' – people who didn't care about Shannan but just jumped on for the ride, a free ride. They didn't care that Shannan had begun using drugs and, by his own admission, was spinning out of control. They didn't care that he had made a living by putting his body on the line. They just wanted his cash and the celebrity. In an interview with *The Sun-Herald* in 2002 Shannan admitted that he had spent over $70 000 on cocaine.

Shannan, or the 'Blaster' as he is known, had been world number one, and he knew that after 97 amateur fights and more than 50 professional fights with only four losses – a professional career that most boxers could only dream of – there was still more in the tank. He knew he could not blow it all away with drugs, wild parties and hanging out with people who didn't care about him or his well-being. So he made some hard decisions and began to do something about his life and the people in it.

Shannan has turned his life around. He found faith in God, and started to talk to kids about the dangers of drugs. In an interview in the *Northern Leader* in 2005 Shannan was quoted as saying, 'My life got way off-track then. My life is so different now. I go to church every Sunday and I go to schools and talk to kids about drug awareness. I'm a different person – when you're on drugs you live in a make-believe world. You think everybody's your friend but really no-one's there for you and nothing is real.'

Today the Blaster believes he has more to live for, especially as he is now the proud dad of Nathalia and because of his newfound passion for teaching kids about drugs, 'I can show kids if you play with drugs, there is no success.'

Shannan Taylor went on to win the world title in the super middleweight division in the World Boxing Federation, and as I write this he is preparing for another world title in the middleweight division, thus aiming to become the first man in history to hold two world titles in the newest world boxing governing body. He also plans to win a third world title in the junior middleweight division.

The Blaster got rid of the 'hangers on', the people who weren't helping him follow his chosen direction in life, the ones who were anchors and dead weights. He is now soaring towards reaching his potential, on track and loving it.

11
Ready for lift-off

If they can make penicillin out of mouldy bread,
they sure can make something out of you.
Muhammad Ali

The transition

Now for the fun part – turning this magnificent balloon,
your magnificent life, from a combination of well-
manufactured components into a glorious flying machine,
soaring majestically into the skies. The transition is never
quick, but it is constant and exciting.

> A man who has no imagination has no wings.
> *Muhammad Ali*

If you have ever seen a hot-air balloon being readied
for flight, you will notice that the process takes a little

time. Once the balloon is assembled, the fuel is ignited, the air is heated and gradually the balloon inflates. Eventually the crew has to hold the basket to the ground while the passengers climb aboard for the ride. The transition is complete. The balloon has gone from being a collection of parts with the potential to fly to a machine capable of flying to great heights.

The key is you have to see your dream as reality before it becomes reality.

It is the same with our lives. We've built the components, assembled them, and gradually our life begins to take the shape we desire. We are about to have lift-off. The key is you have to see your dream as reality before it becomes reality. You have to recognise your potential, your hidden ability to turn your dream into something real.

What is potential?

I'm sure you've heard statements like 'You've got so much potential' or 'Why doesn't she use her potential?' Or even, 'You're oozing potential!' So just what is potential – and how are you oozing it?

Dictionary definitions of potential include 'one's maximum possible level of work or achievement' or 'something that can develop or become actual'. Having potential means that you are capable of achieving things, that your dream is attainable and workable. Note how those words end in 'able'. To have potential means that you are *able*. Able to do what? Whatever your heart desires, that's what!

> Enthusiasm, the sparkle in your eyes,
> the swing in your gait. The grip of your hand,
> the irresistible surge of will and energy to
> execute your ideas.
> *Henry Ford*

Turning potential into reality

So now we've realised that we are 'able' to do what we want to do, the next step is to turn that ability into reality. To do this we have to ultilise something called kinetic energy. Kinetic energy is an energy associated with motion or movement. This tells us that to turn potential ability into reality we have to actually do something! We have to make a decision to act – we have to put our dreams into action. We have gone to the trouble of defining our dreams, making sure our gondola is strong and the connection to the canopy is tight. We have found the right ground crew, know the direction we are heading in and now we just have to take the final step ... and take off!

> Self-esteem is the reputation we acquire
> with ourselves.
> *Nathaniel Branden*

Look out, it's self-doubt!

So, now is the time for our dreams to become realities. But at this point, when our balloon is ready to lift-off, self-doubts may come flooding in. You may start to think that perhaps you won't be able to achieve your dream.

You may be dwelling on your inadequacies, your past failures, the negative experiences you have had, or the negative things people have said about you.

What is self-doubt, anyway?

Self-doubt is when we doubt our own ability to do things. It's a kind of self-destruct mode we can go into if we don't feel confident of our capabilities. Sometimes self-doubt hits us when we are under extreme pressure, like when you sit for an exam, for example. You could read a question that you know the answer to but, because of the examination pressure, you go blank and your mind starts to go into a spin. That's the point where you start to wonder whether you really knew the answer at all! Self-doubt attacks your thinking and can really affect your performance and the way you normally do things.

> Sometimes self-doubt hits us when we are under extreme pressure, like when you sit for an exam, for example.

What do you do about it?

The answer to self-doubt is simple – knock it out! Wipe that self-doubt out! However, this is often easier said than done. When I find myself in situations where self-doubt creeps in, I simply shut my eyes, take a deep breath, and focus on the truth I already know. That I was born a winner, I was born a CHAMPION!

As your dream begins to take shape, take some time to practise dealing with self-doubt. Look at yourself in the mirror at home, in the car, in the toilets at school, university or work, and say out loud, 'I am a winner, born a champion, born from victory, for VICTORY!' Give yourself a champion mindset. Make it a daily habit.

> The man who views the world
> at 50 the same way he did when he was 20
> has wasted 30 years of his life.
> *Muhammad Ali*

Focus on where you are going

Realise that your passion, your desire and your potential, are all greater than people's opinions of you or any of your past mistakes. You have what it takes. Acknowledge your weaknesses, focus on your future, and your dream.

Don't let your past dictate your future. You have a greater future than you have a past.

Don't let your past dictate your future. You have a greater future than you have a past. You don't see people driving cars trying to find their direction by looking in the rear-vision mirror! If they did that they would be in all sorts of bother. It's the same in life. Don't pilot your life looking backwards. Instead, look forward to your future, glancing occasionally at your past to keep mindful of where you came from so you can appreciate where you are going.

Here's how it's done

When I was fighting in the state boxing semi-final titles, I was up against an opponent that was shorter than me, but much more compact. I thought he looked so much stronger than me, so much more menacing. It didn't help that I'd also heard that my opponent had over 50 fights' experience. In the first round I really took care not to get in the way of one of those powerful arms. All I could think was how much it would hurt if I got hit. After dancing around for most of the round avoiding any real encounter, the bell rang. My coach, Don, jumped up onto the platform, leaned into my face and asked, quite sternly, 'Are you finished looking at him?!'

Don then proceeded to remind me of my height and reach advantage, the hard work I had done in the gym, how many times I had sparred against national title holders, all who were much bigger than this guy, so what was I waiting for? He refocused me by reminding me of the truth, as well as reminding me that he believed in me and I was a champion. Needless to say I went on to win the fight very comfortably, and returned the next day to win the championship.

What I've learnt

- Our potential ability can be turned into kinetic energy when we make the decision to put everything we have learnt into practice.
- Turning a dream into reality won't happen overnight. Just like the canopy of a balloon, it takes time to inflate.
- Potential is everything that we can become that we haven't yet acted upon.
- Doubt can cripple us from making that all important decision to act. So don't ignore the doubt, face it and knock it out with the reality that you are a champion, you have what it takes.

The sky is the limit

Robert was a young guy from an ethnic background. He was always told that he was dumb and that he wouldn't amount to anything. Many years ago, during a camp I was running, all the guys sat down and we started talking about our dreams, what we could see ourselves doing in five or ten years time.

Robert said that he dreamed of being an accountant, but his friends always ribbed him for it because he was in the lowest classes at school, and wasn't too good at mathematics.

As a part of our camps, we only encourage and never put down anyone or their dream. All of the boys encouraged Robert and we all said that we believed he could do it. The following year, Robert took that positive experience and began to believe that he could do what was in his heart to do, no matter what anyone said. His grades began to climb rapidly as he applied himself.

We eventually lost contact until recently when we met by chance. Robert informed me that he not only got a job as a chartered accountant, but he eventually started his own business and was quite successful with a number of high-profile clients.

No matter what the dream is, where you want to fly to, how high you want to fly, and how fast you want to get there is up to you. You are your only limitation. So how high do you want to fly?

12
Storm front!

The fight is won or lost well away from witnesses –
behind the lines, in the gym,
out there on the road,
long before I dance under those lights.
Muhammad Ali

You can fight

We're now at the business end of things. We've made the right decisions, our base (gondola) is secure, we have good people (ground crew) around us, the dream (the canopy) is established and in place, all of the passion we have within us is fired up and ready to go, so we have plenty of fuel. We have overcome self-doubt and we have launched our dream! But have you noticed how hard it is to stay on course when you are trying to do something you have never done before?

It is hard to keep your balloon aloft, especially when faced with some stormy weather. This world we live in won't just hand you your dream on a silver platter. You

Not only can you fight, you can win.

will have to fight for it. But you know what? You can fight, you have what it takes. Not only can you fight, you can win. I've learnt a few things about fighting from my career as a boxer, and as a sportsman, and these are principles that can be translated back into everyday life. to help you overcome any storm fronts you may encounter.

> If you can imagine it, you can achieve it.
> If you can dream it, you can become it.
> *William Arthur Ward*

Out for the count

I started my boxing career when I was eighteen. I wanted to fight before that, but my mother wouldn't sign the permission forms so I had to wait until I could sign them myself. After training for almost twelve months at a little local gym, I finally got my chance to compete. It was time to prove myself.

I fought at a local club in front of about 500 people. I was a skinny, 60-kilogram, 181-centimetre lightweight. My opponent had had three fights for three knockout wins. He also weighed about 5 kilograms more than me. I didn't realise what a difference that would make, and my coach had agreed to fight despite the weight difference. He said it wouldn't matter.

I was nervous as hell as I entered the ring. My trainers and friends, Dad and my brother were all there. I was like a cat on a hot tin roof. We received our instructions, touched gloves and waited for the bell. It rang and we moved towards each other. The next thing you know, I'm on the canvas! I thought to myself, 'What are you doing down here? Get up!'

I got to my feet as fast as I could, a little stunned but ready to go on. I fought a rather feeble round but managed to land a few good straight shots and bloodied my opponent's nose. I knew if he didn't stop bleeding the fight would be stopped. I must admit, it was a very nice right hand that got him.

I came out swinging in the second round, aiming for his nose, knowing that it must have been sore. I got him again and again! He started to bleed again and I began to think I had the fight won. But then I became a bit overconfident. I dropped my guard and my opponent dropped me. My next memory was of talking to a doctor who was asking me to count his fingers. I felt ashamed and embarrassed. I quit boxing that night. For three years I wouldn't even go inside a gym.

My next memory was of talking to a doctor who was asking me to count his fingers.

> People grow through experience if they meet life honestly and courageously. This is how character is built.
> *Eleanor Roosevelt*

Get back in the ring

Defeat is one of life's storms. I learnt a humbling lesson from defeat. In boxing there is nowhere to hide. If you are not the better man, if you have not trained, or if you let the emotion of the moment overwhelm you, mark my words, you will pay. It's like that in life as well. Sure, you can hide for a while, you may even start working on your dream, but if you haven't taken care of your base and put in the work to develop your character, you will come crashing down. Even though I had trained my guts out for that fight, paid my money and passed the medical, I still hadn't done all the things I needed to do to make my base strong enough. I had forgotten to remain humble and focused, and so my overconfidence lost me that fight.

> **I was so ashamed of myself for losing the fight that I cut off all contact with the guys at my gym – my trainer, my coach, sparring partners, everyone.**

I was so ashamed of myself for losing the fight that I cut off all contact with the guys at my gym – my trainer, my coach, sparring partners, everyone.

I was so embarrassed. I didn't speak about it for a long time. By the time I was 21 I had let my fitness decline massively. I went from being a state-level swimmer, a four-time state-level surf life-saving competitor, a state-level rugby league player and a state-level sponsored surfer, to being a guy who could barely swim 50 metres. I had met Terrisa in the meantime and we got married, and she became pregnant with our first child Hannah.

I was disgusted by how I had let myself go. But something inside was telling me to get up, just one more time. There was unfinished business to attend to. Ultimately I had a choice to make. I could wallow in my sorrow, or do something about it. So I made a decision to regain my fitness by going down to the local gym and just hit the bags, working up a sweat on a regular basis.

I had moved to a new area by now, well away from anyone who had seen me box previously, so down to the local boxing gym I went. I joined an early group who were training for fitness, nothing else. The competition boxing team trained after us.

At the end of my first session, the trainer offered a sparring session to anyone who was willing. A young guy about my size stepped up, so I thought I'd have a go as well. After all, one thing that never got out of shape was my desire to compete. Knowing how unfit I was, I quickly set the pace by landing a solid combination of punches. Even with headgear on, my sparring partner was soon bleeding from his nose. One thing I always possessed as a boxer was accuracy.

A husky voice rang through the gym. 'Get out of that ring!'

I thought the voice was directed at me so I quickly slipped through the ropes, but then the voice said, 'Not you. Get back in the ring! Get that other kid out.'

The voice belonged to Ross Willis, who was the Australian boxing coach seventeen times. He then put a young 55-kilogram kid in the ring with me and said, 'Give me three rounds.'

I protested that I was very unfit, but Ross would have none of it. Isn't it funny how when we are faced with an opportunity to achieve something we desire, so often we look for excuses and highlight our own weaknesses? This comes from our insecurities and we need to move on from this point, focus on our abilities and make the most of the opportunity in front of us.

I gave Ross his three rounds. Totally exhausted, I was informed that the young guy I just sparred with, and whose lip I had split I might add, was the current 54-kilogram national champion! I was also informed that from now on I would be training with no-one but Ross himself. In three months I would get back in the ring for my next fight. My chance for redemption had presented itself all because of a decision not to run from my shame any more, and to have another go.

> Our greatest weakness lies in giving up.
> The most certain way to succeed is to try
> just one more time.
> *Thomas Edison*

Storms come in all shapes and sizes

Soon after my first fight under Ross, which I won, I had two more fights and ended up with a silver medal in the state titles. Terrisa by this time had just had our second child Joash, and family life was taking up a lot of time.

I searched for approval through sport.

So I retired from boxing, but was itching to remain involved in sport. I still had this burning desire to compete, and more than that I think, to prove myself. I believe this desire to prove myself stems from the lack of approval I received from my father while I was growing up. If we don't receive approval from our fathers or mothers as children, we often spend our life trying to find it elsewhere. Many people I have come across are still trying to prove something to their parents, whether they are doing it through sports or building successful businesses, or doing well at their studies. I searched for approval through sport.

After hanging up the gloves, but still wanting to participate in sport, I saw an article in a local newspaper about the local Metropolitan Cup rugby league side. It was quite a few years since I'd played league but I decided to give it a go.

Training started in late October that year. We had played several trial matches and nine competition games when were all called into the clubhouse for a 'special' team meeting. Everyone was given a letter. The letter started by describing the history of the club and saying how the club was looking forward to a great season with current playing staff. Then the letter read, '… but unfortunately …' You can probably guess the rest.

Due to the salary cap, several players had to be 'let go' from the club and I was one of them. That was disappointing, but what was worse was the fact that at least five guys who I had been running rings around at training and during the games made the team. It was just one more knock down. I then joined a local A-grade side but the team had very little team spirit and poor self-esteem. We didn't win a game and I ended up leaving before season's end because I didn't receive the match payments that were promised, not a single cent!

Life seemed to keep getting the better of me. Every time I tried something I would get so far then fail, or so it seemed. I began wondering why I should bother fighting at all. I just seemed to be going against the flow with everything I did. However, I knew that the state boxing titles were coming up again so I decided to have one more go.

> Failure is simply the opportunity to begin again, this time more intelligently.
> *Henry Ford*

State champion

Although his health was suffering, Ross agreed to coach me for the lead-up fights. I had a fight at a little tournament out in the country and felt I was totally robbed of the decision. I fought hard and clearly landed more shots than my opponent as he was bruised and bleeding, and I was not. But the judges awarded him the split decision. It was Ross's last fight as a coach and I wanted to send him out a winner, but it wasn't to be. Ross then put me onto another coach. He said Don Abnet could take me further than he could. So I joined Don's Magpie Gym. We trained hard for the state titles, competing in the Southern District titles in the lead up. I lost my eighth fight by a split decision to a guy who was, according to all the experts, supposed to knock me out! It was his 154th fight! I then went on to win the state title two weeks later. I became the 1998 state champion for the 63.5-kilogram division. Oh what a feeling! When they hung the medal around my neck I knew that's why I bothered fighting. All of the hard work, all of the defeats, all of the disappointments paled into insignificance, if only for a moment. Because if you get up one more time and keep fighting, eventually you will win. If you keep fighting through all the storm fronts you come across you will be able to keep your dreams in sight.

> When everything seems to be going against you,
> remember that the airplane takes off against
> the wind, not with it.
> *Henry Ford*

A tale of another champion

A good friend of mine, Paul Briggs, is man who has lived the message I'm sharing with you, a man who has fought his way through many a heavy storm. Briggsy is world kickboxing champion and a WBC world lightweight, heavyweight champion.

Paul 'Firepower' Briggs, formerly known as the Hurricane, is an incredibly wise man. After a short time spent in his company you realise he is not your normal boxer. Briggsy had a terrible upbringing with a violent alcoholic father. At an early age he was exposed to things children should never have to experience. He was sexually abused as a young boy, sent overseas to train in a country where he didn't even speak the language, and horribly controlled and manipulated by his father. Along with this, he always played second fiddle to his older brother who was supposed to be the champion in the family. Paul was always just the runt whose role was to provide sparring practice for his brother.

Briggsy went on to overcome all of this and to win a world title. However he then fell into the deep, dark world of rave and dance parties, heavy drugs and even heavier people, one of whom he became! Paul had hit rock bottom when he realised he could do much better than live the life he was now living. He made some hard decisions, took responsibility for his own actions and turned his life around.

Paul Briggs is now one of the most popular professional fighters around the world, commanding television audiences in America of over 50 million viewers every time he fights. He is married with two beautiful children and attracts sponsors who want to be associated with him wherever he goes. He is an example of someone who got up one more time, who didn't give up, and who fought and is fighting the fight for success. He is a true champion. If you want to find out more about his story, I recommend you read his book, *Heart Soul Fire: The Journey of Paul Briggs*.

> Before everything else, getting ready is
> the secret of success.
> *Henry Ford*

Battling storm fronts using the five Ps

With anything that I have achieved in my life, whether it has been sporting events, just going for a surf on my own, business meetings or speaking to audiences, I have learnt that one of the biggest determinants of success is preparation. A rule that I employ in every area of my life is this:

Proper
Preparation
Prevents
Poor
Performance

It might seem pretty obvious, but it's good to say it out loud anyway. If I don't screw the fins into my board and make sure I've given it a fresh wax job, then the next time I go surfing I'll have the worst time of my life, instead of the best. I won't be able to control the board because the fins will probably fall out, and that's presuming I can get to my feet without slipping off because I haven't waxed the board.

If you want to do well at anything – relationships, business, school exams, sporting events, just going for a skate or a surf – you must prepare. Imagine buying a new sports car, deciding at the last minute to go for a weekend drive and not checking the fuel level. You'll soon find yourself pushing that flashy new sports car!

> Train hard, fight easy.
> *Paul Briggs*

Respect others by respecting yourself

Guys and girls, I want you to take heart out of this book. I also want you to realise your worth. Once you realise how valuable you are, you learn to respect yourself. And respecting yourself is a valuable tool to have when you are battling a storm front! Respecting yourself also shows respect to others.

Guys, if you are trying to impress a boss, a coach or a girl, respect is best shown by the effort you put in *before* meeting that person. For instance, if you're going for a job interview, would you rock up in your Adidas trackies, Fubu jumper and the latest Reebok footwear? Would you suck on your last cigarette before you go in for the interview, with a hat on sideways and your boxers on display? Seriously, you may dress like that when hanging out with your friends, but for a job interview? Would *you* consider employing someone if they looked as though they hadn't made any effort to prepare for the interview? I don't think so.

If you are trying to impress a lady, put the effort in. Be a gentleman please. Set a standard worth following. How much you respect girls directly reflects how much you respect yourself. And if you want respect from people, you have to give it first. You can't reap what you haven't sown. If you want tomatoes, plant tomatoes; if you want respect, plant respect.

> The philosophy in the schoolroom in one generation, will be the philosophy of government in the next.
> *Abraham Lincoln*

Ladies, don't think for a second that I've forgotten you. Value yourself when it comes to making decisions about your career. Don't sell yourself short. Always believe in your ability. That also goes in the arena of sports as well. If you want to excel and be the best you can be, whether you end up representing your country or you want to play well in local competition, then believe in your own value and the value you can bring to a team. Believe in the level of competitiveness you will bring to your competition. Value yourself!

If you are looking for Mr Right to come along, the best way to find him is to respect yourself. You are worth respecting, you are special, precious, and worthy of honour. So honour yourself and your body. If a young man doesn't try to win your affection by investing his time and showing you respect, then don't give yourself to him cheaply; he doesn't deserve your friendship.

Gattaca

About ten years ago I watched a movie called *Gattaca*. The movie is set in the not-too-distant future where people can have designer babies. Imperfect genes and genetic defaults are removed to produce perfect babies, all via the test tube. How convenient!

In the movie a child conceived in the old-fashioned way is called an 'in-valid'. Ethan Hawke plays a character called Vincent Freeman who is one of the last in-valids. He dreams of becoming an astronaut with the Gattaca space agency, but because he was born with a weak heart the agency will not accept him. However Vincent never gives up hope. He strikes a deal with a 'valid' who has become crippled through a car accident, and by illegally impersonating him, he eventually finds his way into the space program.

Vincent has a 'valid' younger brother, Anton, who is a police officer. Anton investigates an apparent breach in the space program security and discovers his weak, 'in-valid' brother blitzing the program. When they were growing up, the brothers would have swimming races which Anton, with his stronger heart, would always win. The race would be like a game of chicken. Swim out from the shore as far and as fast as you can, and the first one to turn around lost. However, in one race, Vincent beat his stronger, younger brother. They never raced again after that. But as the story unfolds, Anton uncovers his brother's ruse to get into the space program. He steps in to stop Vincent from fulfilling his lifelong dream to fly into space on one of the Gattaca space ships. In a last-bid effort to prove his worthiness to be an astronaut, Vincent challenges his younger brother to one more swimming race in the sea.

As the two race toward the horizon, Anton begins to fall behind. Vincent challenges him several times to give up and eventually he does. But the younger brother with the stronger heart is desperate to find out how Vincent beat him. The answer is awesome. Vincent says, 'I left nothing for the return to shore.'

To prove he is worthy, Vincent was prepared to drown! His dream was worth fighting for.

> The mediocre mind is incapable of understanding the man who refuses to bow blindly to conventional prejudices and chooses to instead express his opinions courageously and honestly.
> *Albert Einstein*

A lesson from the past

Fighting the fight for your dream is worth it, because you are worth it. And who knows, you might just make history. Abraham Lincoln did!

Born in Kentucky in 1809, Lincoln worked many jobs, beginning as a flat-boatman, then a postmaster, a storekeeper, a surveyor and a rail splitter before becoming a lawyer. In 1830 his business failed, in 1832 he lost his bid to be elected to the Illinois legislature, and in 1833 his business failed again! In 1834 he did succeed in being elected to the Illinois legislature but two years later he suffered a nervous breakdown. In 1838 he was nominated for the position of speaker and lost, and then lost again five years later when he was nominated for Congress. This man did not give up on his dream though, and in 1846 he was elected to Congress. But in 1848 he lost re-nomination for Congress. He then failed to be appointed as a commissioner of the general lands in 1849. He was defeated for the United States Senate in 1854 and defeated for nomination for Vice-President in 1856, then again defeated for the Senate in 1858.

However, in 1860, Abraham Lincoln became the sixteenth president of the United States of America. His total formal education amounted to one year!

> Generations to come will scarcely believe
> that such a one as this walked the earth
> in flesh and blood.
> *Albert Einstein*

What I've learnt

- You have what it takes to overcome storms on your way to achieving your dream.
- A champion is not one who doesn't get knocked down. A champion is one who gets up, one more time.
- Poor performances are avoided by proper preparation.
- If respect is not given to oneself first, it will be hard to receive it from anyone else. If you respect yourself others will too.
- We can find lessons for our future in the past.

Storms on many fronts: Winston Churchill

Sir Winston Churchill wrote six massive volumes about the Second World War. He called the first book *The Gathering Storm*. Apart from the huge storm that was the Second World War, Churchill faced many storms in his lifetime.

Born in 1874 he attended the Royal Military College at Sandhurst and encountered his first big storms at the start of his military career when he saw action on the north-west frontier in India and then in the Sudan. He faced another storm while he was working as a journalist in the Boer War and was captured and made a prisoner-of-war.

In 1900 he became a conservative member of parliament but encountered another storm when he became disaffected with the Tory party in 1904 and joined the Liberal Party. The Liberals won the election in 1905 and Churchill was appointed undersecretary at the Colonial Office. Always a man of action, he entered Cabinet in 1908 as president of the Board of Trade and went on to become Home Secretary in 1910.

The following year he became First Lord of the Admiralty. He held this position until the storms of the First World War rolled in, resigning after he was blamed for the disaster in the Dardanelles. He then joined the army serving for a time on the Western Front. In 1917 he returned to government as Minister of Munitions. From 1919–1921 he was Secretary of State for War and Air, and from 1924–1929 Chancellor of the Exchequer.

Over the next decade he kept walking into storms. His opposition to Indian self-rule and his support for Edward VIII during the abdication crisis made him unpopular and because of this his warnings about the rise of Nazi Germany and the need for British rearmament were ignored. Churchill again became First Lord of the Admiralty when war broke out in 1939, then Prime Minister in May of 1940. He was about to face his biggest storm.

Churchill's refusal to surrender to Nazi Germany inspired his nation, and he built strong ties with US President Roosevelt while maintaining an alliance with the Soviet Union. He lost power in 1945 but remained Opposition leader and regained power in 1951. In 1953 he won the Nobel Prize for literature. He resigned as Prime Minister in 1955 but remained as a member of parliament until shortly before his death in 1965.

Me and my Gift

x

GORDON HAD A GIFT.

A PRICELESS GIFT
THAT COULD HAVE
CHANGED HISTORY.

IN 73 YEARS
GORDON NEVER ONCE
OPENED HIS GIFT.

HE SHOWED
GREAT RESTRAINT.

... THEN HE DIED.

13
Make the most of it

There is nothing more painful,
than living with regret.
No Fear clothing company

Maintain focus and don't hold back

As life unfolds there will be many opportunities, threats, temptations and illusions which could take your focus off your dream. One small bit of advice I would give you is to stay the course, maintain your focus on the thing that drives you. Rays of sunlight focused through a magnifying glass can create a massive bushfire. Focus has this power. Stay focused on your dream with heart and mind and you will be amazed at what you can achieve.

The next thing I would challenge you with is to not hold back. Just like Vincent Freeman in *Gattaca*, leave nothing for the return trip. Chase your dream, and live your dream with everything you have. You will enjoy the ride knowing that you have put everything into it.

It doesn't get any easier

I hate it when I hear someone telling a young person it will get easier as they get older. What a load of rot! Life doesn't get any easier as you get older. At school, if you don't do your homework, the worst punishment you may get is detention. But what happens if you don't do your assignments at university? Sure, there's no punishment as such, but bludge there, and you won't get that credential you need to help you fulfil your dream. What about the workplace? That's simple! Bludge there and it's hasta la vista, baby, see you later. A boss will simply show you the door! Not many dreams get fulfilled living on welfare payments. I have never met a person who bludges all the time who is truly fulfilled. So do the work now because it *doesn't* get any easier.

> To achieve your goals and dreams, you have to grow. The rate at which you grow is up to you. You have a choice in all of this, and that's pretty cool.

> He who has never learned to obey
> cannot be a good commander.
> *Aristotle*

As we get older, more is required of us and, as I said, it doesn't get any easier. But you gradually grow into your responsibilities. To achieve your goals and dreams, you have to grow. The rate at which you grow is up to you. You have a choice in all of this, and that's pretty cool. You can stay young, inexperienced and irresponsible as you get older, *or* you can take the bull by the horns and get out there and live your dream. But have fun while you're doing it – the higher you go, the harder the challenge, the greater the reward!

Tough it out

Life is tough. It is also what you make of it. Guess what? In a real world, good things happen to bad people, and bad things happen to good people. It is no-one's fault, it is just life, and we are right in the middle of it. We can set our *own* course or we can be pulled along by the wind and be taken wherever it chooses. Doing that is easy. Sailing into the wind on rough seas is a challenge that takes all sorts of skill and courage. You don't become a good sailor floating on a pond. You get out in the open sea, take on the storms and challenges that life throws at you. You can do it!

> **We can set our *own* course or we can be pulled along by the wind and be taken wherever it chooses.**

> The ultimate measure of a man is not where he stands in times of comfort, but where stands at times of challenge and controversy.
> *Martin Luther King Jnr*

I believe in people. I think that no matter what we have been through, we are all called to greatness. We all have a choice to make as to how we approach life: do we whinge or do we win? The only person who can make that choice is you. So choose wisely! Everybody faces adversity. You can let it either swallow you up or inspire you to a new level, a new dimension of living.

> Don't follow where the path may lead.
> Go instead where there is no path and leave a trail.
> *Harold R McAlindon*

It's attitude that counts

Life is something that you cannot always control. Some people try very hard to control everything and everyone around them, but they try in vain. However there is one thing that you have total control over, and this is your attitude. Your attitude influences the way you respond or react to life and the adversities and successes it throws your way. If life hands you a lemon, do you suck on it? Or do you turn that lemon into cool delicious lemonade? The choice is yours.

> Let him who would be moved to convince others be first moved to convince himself.
> *Thomas Carlyle*

Life can be a pile of manure at times. It can throw up lots of negatives. But with the right attitude you can use every experience, negative or positive, as a building block to achieve what you want out of life. What you do when a pile of manure is dumped on you is up to you. Do you complain and sook about it, moaning about the person who was responsible for dumping it on you? Do you become part of the rotting pile, part of the garbage? There is another choice. You can view that manure as fertiliser, and use it to grow the most beautiful and most colourful roses known to man.

So what will it be – manure or fertiliser? Make every experience worth something to you. Learn from it. If you make a mistake, don't do it again; think of alternatives. Whether you experience a tremendous victory or a soul-crushing defeat, learn from that experience. You probably don't realise how experienced you already are!

> **If you make a mistake, don't do it again; think of alternatives.**

Stuff yourself silly

We cannot control what happens to us all the time. Not every experience we have is of our doing. But we can be aware of our surroundings; we can be alert to what is happening around us. I'm trying to empower you to live a proactive life rather than a reactive one. To become a positive person, if you are not one already, or to become more positive than you are already, takes effort and self-discipline. But it's not the sort of discipline that hurts. No, it's really a whole lot of fun.

Life is a smorgasbord. It is full of wonder and adventure. This world is full of wonderful people and personalities and experiences. Stuff yourself silly on them. When I used to go to those 'all you can eat' restaurants, I used to interpret that as '*more* than you can eat'. That's how we need to see life. Get out there with a 'more than you can eat' attitude. Why don't we look for every possible experience we can? Why not gorge ourselves on life, and make the most of it?

> **Why don't we look for every possible experience we can? Why not gorge ourselves on life, and make the most of it?**

Life is far too short to be lived with envy or unforgiveness, and we only get one shot at it. So have a blast. Take a huge plate full of all the differently flavoured experiences out there and stuff yourself. Eat until you can't eat any more, then go back for dessert. Life is full of great tastes. You may not like everything you try, but how will you know what you do like unless you have a taste test? Don't be someone who thinks that they have to exist on a diet of mouldy bread and dirty water. Don't be a prisoner to some false idea that you can't do anything, that you are only a beggar. You, my friend, were born for greatness. You are a ruler of your world. Step up to your destiny and take your fill. Go on, live with the 'more than you can eat' attitude. Make the most of it!

> Imagination is more important than knowledge. Knowledge is limited. Imagination encircles the world.
> *Albert Einstein*

What I've learnt

- Concentrated focus is a powerful thing. Everyday sunlight can become a raging fire if focused in one direction.

- Life doesn't get easier. Give it everything you've got, now!
- How you experience life depends on your attitude.
- Negative experiences can be turned into positive opportunities: it's your choice.
- Have a 'more than you can eat' attitude toward life – every day can be a smorgasbord of learning experiences.

Determination breeds a winner: Layne Beachley

Layne was born in Australia in 1972. She was adopted by the Beachley family who lived in the Sydney beachside suburb of Manly. Layne thrived on competitive sport as a youngster, especially tennis, before the beach lifestyle, and surfing in particular, took over her life completely.

At sixteen the skinny, determined young surfer decided she wanted to make her mark in a sport dominated by men. So she bypassed the amateur contests and went straight to the professional ranks, surfing in trial events around Australia. However, it wasn't made easy for her as she had to fight for her spot in the waves to practise. The established surfers, particularly the males, gave her a really hard time. This only made Layne more determined to show them what she could do. By the time she was twenty, she was ranked number six in the world. Layne then began a training regime that was so intense it set her apart from every other female competitor in the surfing world and laid a solid foundation for big-wave riding.

However, Layne suffered two major setbacks when she became ill with chronic fatigue syndrome in 1993 and again in 1996. In order to get well she was placed on a yeast-free, wheat-free, sugar-free, dairy-free and fruit-free diet, and ordered to rest. It was an extremely difficult time for Layne because she wasn't allowed to train or surf. In fact, at times, Layne thought she may never be able to surf at an elite level again. However, with support from her friends, she slowly began to recover. As Layne says, 'At moments like those you surround yourself with really positive people, people that love you and support you and people that build you back up.'

In 1996, when she had eventually recovered from her second bout of chronic fatigue, Layne won the women's event on the huge waves at Hawaii's Sunset Beach. In 1998 she won what would be the first of seven consecutive world titles, the most consecutive world titles won by a woman or a man in the history of surfing.

In 2003 Layne launched Aim for the Stars, a foundation which helps young women make their dreams come true. The foundation was born from Layne's desire to help young women who were struggling financially to support their goals, just as she had often struggled during her career.

Layne Beachley has made the most of the difficult situations she has come across in life. She has learnt from them and grown stronger because of them, thus becoming the extraordinarily successful person she is today.

EVERY NOW AND THEN
DAVO FELT THE URGE
TO EXERCISE HIS
SUPERHUMAN POWERS

BUT LOTS OF PRACTICE
MADE IT POSSIBLE TO
CONTROL THESE URGES
AND SIT DOWN AGAIN

14
Firestorm

You can have everything in life you want if you
just give enough other people what they want.

Zig Ziglar

Momentum

Momentum is a great word. Momentum is the power to move forward at an ever-increasing pace. It is the drive or thrust which carries you forward. It is a powerful thing to have in your life.

There comes a time when your dreams need to power forward under their own steam if you are to become all you are meant to be. As we have already talked about, fulfilling our dreams is a lot like flying a hot-air balloon. To ready a balloon for lift-off, many preparations have to take place. Then when the engines are fired up, it takes an incredible amount of energy, power and fuel to get that baby off the ground. Once the balloon is airborne, it still takes a lot of energy to build momentum to get to a safe cruising altitude, but when the balloon is on course, only little bursts of thrust are needed to maintain its course.

> One of the greatest discoveries a man makes, one of his greatest surprises, is to find he can do what he was afraid he couldn't do.
> *Henry Ford*

The same is true of your dream. You will find as you gain momentum and start heading into the wild blue yonder with your dream that other things will sort themselves out. For example, deals are made more easily, contracts start to get signed regularly, sponsors come on board and the financial backing you need starts to become a steady flow rather than the sporadic dripping you've been used to, all that sort of thing. And as you head off into the sky, like-minded people will gather around you. By being positive you will attract positive people to you.

My advice at this point is 'Don't settle for a slow speed'. Gain as much momentum as you can. It will take a little more effort, but the faster you go, the further you will travel, and the more fun you will have along the way.

> Learn from yesterday, live for today, hope for tomorrow.
> The important thing is to not stop questioning.
> *Albert Einstein*

Get a top crew

In order to get this far you will have gathered a strong group of supporters around you. These are the people who will have helped you take off.

How will you spot someone that is right for your crew? That's pretty easy, I reckon. They will want to serve you and most of the time they will do it for free, especially when you are starting. You'll know when the right members of your crew rock up. This sounds like the most impractical business advice anyone can give, but it works for me: trust your gut, go with your heart!

You will discover that bringing others along on your journey is the most rewarding aspect of fulfilling your dream. A good way to gauge whether your dream is a success or not and whether you are a success or not is to ask yourself this question: 'How many people am I helping to succeed?'

This sounds like the most impractical business advice anyone can give, but it works for me: trust your gut, go with your heart!

Sir Richard Branson is a good case in point. Through his success with the Virgin label, he has helped the dreams of countless people come to pass. Brett Godfrey, the head of Virgin Blue Airlines in Australia, is just one example. He dreamed of running a national low-cost airline in Australia. Sir Richard believed in him and launched Virgin Blue with Brett Godfrey overseeing all operations.

Positive peer pressure

Peer group pressure is a powerful phenomenon. Its effects are largely recognised in schools around the world, but it also operates in the corporate world, in sporting communities and in political circles. Peer group pressure is everywhere. People want to be accepted. Acceptance is a natural human need and desire. It is vital for our survival.

The term 'peer group pressure' has a negative connotation, and there is a good reason for this: people do all kinds of crazy and often immature things just to 'fit in'. I did in my teenage years. Firstly it was smoking cigarettes, and then it was pot. Then I got involved in some crazy stunts to see who of us had 'balls', you know, courage! When I was fourteen and desperate to fit in and be accepted, I wanted to join in an 'elite' group of *special* surfboard riders called the 'Mongrel Dogz'. To be accepted into this group you had to pass an initiation test. This was an interesting challenge where two members of the gang would take one of your arms each, sink their teeth into them and bite as hard as they could for as long as they wanted. If they didn't draw blood it had to be done again, and if you shed a tear or screamed you didn't pass the test.

That is a classic example of negative peer pressure. But what about positive peer pressure? This is something that I endeavour to instil in every environment I encounter. I try to create an atmosphere where colleagues are pleased for their workmates when they close a really big deal, or where people celebrate a friend's success and use it as inspiration to spur themselves on to achieve great things. It is vital to establish a peer pressure system where encouragement is cool and where bagging each

negatives, become the positive. Look at your life. You have so much to give this world; there is so much passion inside you. If the world around you has beaten you into submission, use that experience to ignite your passion. Knock out the doubts about yourself and your future. They all deserve a punch in the head. The doubts that is! Definitely not the people! Doubts steal joy from you and rob you of your possibilities. Knock them out!

Become a firestorm! Get 'so' on fire that everyone who comes into contact with you walks away ablaze with hope and a vision of their own. People love to be around positive life-affirming personalities. They are fun to be with. Life is meant to be fun, enjoyed, experienced and lived. Work in teams with others; connect with people, don't use them. They will enjoy you and you will enjoy them and friendships will be made that could last a lifetime.

The only time you fail is when you quit.

Ignite your passion, get your dream airborne, and fly it to wherever you want to go. The sky is the limit. Aim for the stars without fear of failure. The only time you fail is when you quit. If you aim for the stars and land on the moon, at least you reached outer space.

I want to leave you with this thought. Always remember it, especially when going through tough times.

Greater is the force within you than the obstacles before you.

The force within you is your potential, your calling. It is where your dreams come from, and where all of your passion finds its genesis. That force can, and will, make you a ground breaker, a history maker, a planet shaker! Go on, I dare you – live your dream! Give yourself permission to fly!

What I've learnt

- Momentum is a key factor in making a dream become a reality.
- It takes more energy and force to see a dream lift-off than it does to keep it on course.
- Part of your success is helping others to succeed.
- Positive peer group pressure makes a huge difference. Everyone can benefit from another's success.
- We can ignite the dreams of those around us. You can become a firestorm.

The power of the positive: Ernest Shackleton

Ernest Shackleton was one of the most positive leaders I have ever heard of. For him and his crew to survive their ill-fated expedition to the Antarctic aboard the *Endurance*, he had to be!

Born in Kilkea, County Kildare, in southern Ireland in 1874, he was the son of a farmer turned doctor. Preferring the idea of heading out to sea rather than studying medicine as his father wished, he joined the merchant navy when he was sixteen. During his early career he went to the Antarctic on an expedition led by Captain Robert Scott. In 1908 he returned on the whaling ship *Nimrod*, leading his own expedition. He and his men made it to within 156 kilometres of the South Pole, the furthest south anyone had ever been. Shackleton turned back to save the lives of his men, something he would later become famous for doing again.

In 1914 Sir Ernest Shackleton set off on his most famous Antarctic expedition. The plan was to cross the Antarctic continent from the Weddell Sea to the Ross Sea via the Pole, a distance of some 2896 kilometres. Early in 1915, just one day's sailing from the continent; the *Endurance* became trapped in pack ice. Eleven months later, in November 1915, the *Endurance* was finally squashed and sank. Preparing his men for an arduous trek to the mainland, Shackleton issued an order that each man could take only 2 pounds of personal items (a little less than a kilogram) with them. As an example to the others, Shackleton discarded his gold watch, a gold cigarette case and several gold sovereigns.

The optimism and good leadership that Shackleton

displayed throughout the amazing feat of human endurance that followed has become legendary. 'He never appears to be anything but the acme of good humour and hopefulness,' wrote one of the expedition's scientists, Thomas Orde-Lees, in his diary. Shackleton's encouragement and optimism and the even-handed discipline he showed to both officers and seamen set alight a fire of belief in his crew that would ultimately save their lives.

The men had to set up camp on the ice floes. They lived on penguins and seals until in the end they were forced to kill their beloved sled dogs. Two abortive attempts to march to the mainland tested Shackleton's leadership but he was able to encourage his men to carry on as a disciplined unit.

By 16 April 1916, the end of the Southern Hemisphere summer, the ice had melted so much that the men were forced to take to three life rafts. Suffering from dysentery they rowed for a week until luckily they reached Elephant Island off the tip of the Antarctic Peninsular. Knowing that if they all stayed on this barren island of rock and ice they would surely die, Shackleton and five others set off to the island of South Georgia in a 6.7-metre long lifeboat, the *James Caird*, in a make or break effort to seek help. They encountered a hurricane and mountainous waves. They rowed for seventeen days covering a distance of nearly 1300 kilometres. To this day their journey is regarded as the most dangerous small boat journey ever undertaken.

Shackleton, Captain Frank Worsley and second officer Tom Crean then had to trek 35 kilometres across the uncharted interior of the mountainous island to reach the Stromness whaling station before the weather closed in. They just made it in time and the three men who had remained on the other side of South Georgia were picked up shortly afterwards.

Shackleton was desperate to rescue the rest of his loyal crew. Three times the ice held him back but on the fourth attempt he succeeded in rescuing his men. When he reached Elephant Island aboard a Chilean ship on 30 August 1916, he discovered that every man was alive. Against all the odds, every member of the expedition survived!

It was Sir Ernest Shackleton's positive, encouraging, optimistic leadership that gave his men hope and the will to survive. Their fires were lit by the firestorm who led them.

Acknowledgements

I have some solid, supportive ground crew members in my life, beginning with my wife Terrisa. You are the best. Nothing means anything without you. My three awesome children, Hannah, Joash and Micah, you guys always encourage me. Other great crew members include my mate Brett; my operations manager Thomas; my mum, who is always there to help and is never anything but supportive – no negative comment ever comes from her; Mark Priest and Don Malvenan who paid for our first trip to Western Samoa; Al Paddison who paid for our Kokoda adventure; Brett and Tess who have always been supportive; Adam Shand who is always ready to provide business advice, connections to people, including those in the media, and, most of all, friendship; Churchy and Chris at Mac Fields, Bev Baker from Mac Bank, and Mick and Ronda who helped us out financially when we were really struggling. To all my ground crew, what can I say but thank you so much.

I would also like to say a very special thank you to the team at Finch publishing: Sam, for your tireless efforts with editing and helping me with all the fine tunning with the concept of the book, your understanding and positive pressure with deadlines, you rock; Jane, for the enormous efforts in editing; Carol, for your professionalism and enthusiasm with the media and marketing, you do such a wonderful job, and of course Rex, thank you so much for believing in me and putting your faith and name to my writing – how can I ever thank you enough? Thank you all so much, you are all a very important part of my ground crew.

Recommended reading

Biddulph, Steve. *Manhood: An action plan for changing men's lives*, Finch Publishing, 1994.

Biddulph, Steve. *Raising Boys: Why boys are different – and how to help them become happy and well-balanced men*, Finch Publishing, 1994.

Briggs, Paul. *Heart, Soul, Fire: The journey of Paul Briggs*, HarperCollins, 2005.

Cole, Edwin, Lewis. *On Becoming a Real Man*, Thomas Nelson Publishers, 1992.

Cole, Edwin, Lewis. *Maximized Manhood: A guide to family survival*, Whitaker House Publishers, 1982.

Cole, Edwin, Lewis. *Courage: Winning life's tough battles*, Honor Books.

Eldredge, John. *Wild at Heart: Discovering the secrets of a man's soul*, Thomas Nelson Publishers, 2001.

Scanlon, Paul. *I am not my Father*: Abundant Life Publishing, 2007.

Other Finch titles of interest

Acting From the Heart
Australian advocates for asylum seekers tell their stories
Edited by Sarah Mares and Louise Newman
This powerful and heart-rending collection of stories highlights the dark side of refugee and asylum seeker policy in Australia. In *Acting from the Heart*, over 50 people who reflect the diversity of this movement describe how and why they became involved. ISBN 978 1876451 783

Blood Ties
The stories of five positive women
Edited by Salli Trathen
This collection of the stories of five Australian HIV-positive women reveals how each woman approached her predicament, and the inner qualities she drew on to persevere. The authors' honest and courageous writing allows us to live with them through their struggles. What emerges is a triumph of the human spirit over adversity. ISBN 978 1876451 295

The Other Side of Blue
What we learn through overcoming adversity
Edited by Michael Colling
The Other Side of Blue is an anthology of 20 Australian stories from people in their 20s and 30s that provide hope for those struggling with tough issues in their lives. The contributions span many daunting and complex challenges: from surviving childhood sexual abuse, to family breakdowns, 'coming out', domestic violence, depression, recovery from severe injury and coping with the death of a loved one. For those who are finding life tough, these stories show that you're not alone: others have also faced these things and survived. ISBN: 9781 876451 813

Bully Blocking
Six secrets to help children deal with teasing and bullying
Evelyn Field
Evelyn Field reveals the 'six secrets of bully blocking', which contain important life skills for any young person. Activities introduce young readers to new skills in communicating feelings, responding to stressful situations and building a support network. An empowering book for parents and their children (5–16 years). ISBN 978 1876451 776

Emotional Fitness
Facing yourself, facing the world
Cynthia Morton
Cynthia Morton outlines her innovative program of 30 'emotional workouts', which helps individuals learn how to overcome difficult issues in their lives, care for themselves and ultimately reach self-acceptance. They are tailored for different stages along the path to emotional recovery and have been successfully used in sessions with individuals and groups. ISBN 978 1876451 585

Getting on with Others
How to teach your child essential social skills
John Cooper
Cooperative children do better at school and in life; they learn how to make friends, manage their emotions and solve problems with others. John Cooper, who has 30 years of clinical practice working with children and families, shows how parents can teach these skills. ISBN 978 1876451 691

Girls' Talk
Young women speak their hearts and minds (2nd edition)
Dr Maria Pallotta-Chiarolli
In the new edition of this landmark book, girls inspire us with their honesty about friendships, family life, love, sexuality, body issues, prejudice, their struggles and their dreams. ISBN 978 1876451 707

The Happiness Handbook
Strategies for a happy life (2nd edition)
Dr Timothy Sharp
In this updated edition, Dr Sharp introduces his latest and most powerful tool: the CHOOSE Model, which incorporates all the latest research on positive psychology in a practical and easy-to-follow guide. Dr Sharp is the founder of the Happiness Institute in Australia and author of *The Good Sleep Guide*. ISBN 987 1876451 790

Journeys in Healing
How others have triumphed over disease and disability
Dr Shaun Matthews

Dr Shaun Matthews takes us into the lives of eight people who have suffered life-altering illness or disability. Their stories present empowering messages for all sufferers of disease and disability, and demonstrate the interconnectedness between physical, mental, emotional and spiritual health. ISBN 978 1876451 424

Life Smart
Choices for young people about friendship, family and future
Vicki Bennett
This highly acclaimed book for teenagers provides a valuable perspective and sound advice on how to deal with the most pressing issues of those vital years – the ups and downs of friendship and love, learning to accept ourselves and others, creating a direction in our lives, and relating to our families. ISBN 978 1876451 134

Manhood
An action plan for changing men's lives (3rd edition)
Steve Biddulph
Steve Biddulph tackles the key areas of a man's life – parenting, love and sexuality, finding meaning in work, and making real friends. He presents new pathways to healing the past and forming true partnerships with women, as well as honouring our own inner needs. ISBN 978 1876451 202

Raising Boys
Why boys are different – and how to help them become happy and well-balanced men (2nd edition)
Steve Biddulph
In this international bestseller, Steve Biddulph looks at the most important issues in boys development from birth to manhood and discusses the warm, strong parenting and guidance that boys need. *Raising Boys* considers issues such as: how mothers teach boys about life and love; the way testosterone changes behaviour; the five essentials that fathers provide; how boys[1] brains are different; understanding the three stages of boyhood; and helping boys learn a caring attitude towards sex. Steve Biddulph, a leading family therapist, author and speaker, has been at the forefront of change during the last two decades with this groundbreaking, international success.
ISBN 978 1876 451 509

Index